INTERNATIONAL CONFLICT IN THE TWENTIETH CENTURY
TWENTIETH CENTURY
A Christian View

RELIGIOUS PERSPECTIVES
Planned and Edited by
RUTH NANDA ANSHEN

RELIGIOUS PERSPECTIVES · VOLUME TWO

INTERNATIONAL CONFLICT IN THE TWENTIETH CENTURY

A Christian View

by Herbert Butterfield

GREENWOOD PRESS, PUBLISHERS
WESTPORT, CONNECTICUT

Library of Congress Cataloging in Publication Data

Butterfield, Sir Herbert, 1900-
    International conflict in the twentieth century.

    Reprint of the ed. published by Harper, New York,
which was issued as v. 2 of Religious perspectives.
    1. International relations. 2. Christianity and
international affairs. I. Title. II. Series: Religious perspectives, v. 2.
[JX1395.B87 1974]   327   74-6777
ISBN 0-8371-7569-0

RELIGIOUS PERSPECTIVES
Volume I: *The Historic Reality of Christian Culture,*
by Christopher Dawson

Originally published in 1960 by Harper & Brothers
Publishers, New York

Reprinted with the permission of Harper & Row, Publishers, Inc.

Reprinted in 1974 by Greenwood Press,
a division of Williamhouse-Regency Inc.

Library of Congress Catalog Card Number 74-6777

ISBN 0-8371-7569-0

Printed in the United States of America

CONTENTS

Religious Perspectives:
Its Meaning and Purpose 7

Preface 13

Introduction 15

1. Morality and the Way We Stage the Conflict 21

2. The Scientific Method in the Realm of Politics 39

3. History and the Possibility of a *Détente* 59

4. Human Nature and the Dominion of Fear 79

5. Christianity and Global Revolution 99

Index 121

RELIGIOUS PERSPECTIVES
Its Meaning and Purpose

RELIGIOUS PERSPECTIVES represents a quest for the rediscovery of man. It constitutes an effort to define man's search for the essence of being in order that he may have a knowledge of goals. It is an endeavor to show that there is no possibility of achieving an understanding of man's total nature on the basis of phenomena known by the analytical method alone. It hopes to point to the false antinomy between revelation and reason, faith and knowledge, grace and nature, courage and anxiety. Mathematics, physics, philosophy, biology and religion, in spite of their almost complete independence, have begun to sense their interrelatedness and to become aware of that mode of cognition which teaches that "the light is not without but within me, and I myself am the light."

Modern man is threatened by a world created by himself. He is faced with the conversion of mind to naturalism, a dogmatic secularism and an opposition to a belief in the transcendent. He begins to see, however, that the universe is given not as one existing and one perceived but as the unity of subject and object; that the barrier between them cannot be said to have been dissolved as the result of recent experience in the physical sciences, since this barrier has never existed. Confronted with the question of meaning, he is summoned to rediscover and scrutinize the immutable and the permanent which constitute the dynamic, unifying aspect of life as well as the principle of differentiation; to reconcile identity and diversity, immutability and unrest. He begins to recognize that just as every person descends by his particular path, so he is able to ascend, and this ascent aims at a return to the source of creation, an inward home from which he has become estranged.

It is the hope of RELIGIOUS PERSPECTIVES that the rediscovery of man will point the way to the rediscovery of God. To this end a rediscovery of first principles should constitute part of the quest. These principles, not to be superseded by new discoveries, are not those of historical worlds that come to be and perish. They are to be sought in the heart and spirit of man, and no interpretation of a merely historical or scientific universe can guide the search. RELIGIOUS PERSPECTIVES attempts not only to ask dispassionately what the nature of God is, but also to restore to human life at least the hypothesis of God and the symbols that relate to him. It endeavors to show that man is faced with the metaphysical question of the truth of religion while he encounters the empirical question of its effects on the life of humanity and its meaning for society. Religion is here distinguished from theology and its doctrinal forms and is intended to denote the feelings, aspirations and acts of men, as they relate to total reality.

RELIGIOUS PERSPECTIVES is nourished by the spiritual and intellectual energy of world thought, by those religious and ethical leaders who are not merely spectators but scholars deeply involved in the critical problems common to all religions. These thinkers recognize that human morality and human ideals thrive only when set in a context of a transcendent attitude toward religion and that by pointing to the ground of identity and the common nature of being in the religious experience of man, the essential nature of religion may be defined. Thus, they are committed to re-evaluate the meaning of everlastingness, an experience which has been lost and which is the content of that *visio Dei* constituting the structure of all religions. It is the many absorbed everlastingly into the ultimate unity, a unity subsuming what Whitehead calls the fluency of God and the everlastingness of passing experience.

These volumes will seek to show that the unity of which we speak consists in a certitude emanating from the nature of man who seeks God and the nature of God who seeks man. Such certitude bathes in an intuitive act of cognition, participating in the divine essence and is related to the natural spirituality of intelligence. This is not by any means to say that there is an equivalence of all faiths in the traditional religions of human history. It is, however, to emphasize the distinction between the spiritual and the temporal which all religions acknowledge. For duration of thought is composed of instants superior to time, and is an intuition of the permanence of existence and its metahistorical reality. In fact, the symbol* itself found on cover and jacket of each volume of RELIGIOUS PERSPECTIVES is the visible sign or representation of the essence, immediacy and timelessness of religious experience; the one immutable center, which may be analogically related to Being in pure act, moving with centrifugal and ecu-

---

* From the original design by Leo Katz.

menical necessity outward into the manifold modes, yet simulta-
neously, with dynamic centripetal power and with full intentional
energy, returning to the source. Through the very diversity of its
authors, the Series will show that the basic and poignant concern
of every faith is to point to, and overcome the crisis in our apoca-
lyptic epoch—the crisis of man's separation from man and of
man's separation from God—the failure of love. The authors will
endeavor, moreover, to illustrate the truth that the human heart
is able, and even yearns, to go to the very lengths of God; that
the darkness and cold, the frozen spiritual misery of recent time,
are breaking, cracking and beginning to move, yielding to efforts
to overcome spiritual mutness and moral paralysis. In this way,
it is hoped, the immediacy of pain and sorrow, the primacy of
tragedy and suffering in human life, may be transmuted into a
spiritual and moral triumph.

RELIGIOUS PERSPECTIVES is therefore an effort to explore the
meaning of God, an exploration which constitutes an aspect of
man's intrinsic nature, part of his ontological substance. The
Series grows out of an abiding concern that in spite of the release of man's creative energy which science has in part accom-
plished, this very science has overturned the essential order of
nature. Shrewd as man's calculations have become concerning
his means, his choice of ends which was formerly correlated with
belief in God, with absolute criteria of conduct, has become wit-
less. God is not to be treated as an exception to metaphysical
principles, invoked to prevent their collapse. He is rather their
chief exemplification, the source of all potentiality. The personal
reality of freedom and providence, of will and conscience, may
demonstrate that "he who knows" commands a depth of consciousness inaccessible to the profane man, and is capable of that
transfiguration which prevents the twisting of all good to igno-
miny. This religious content of experience is not within the prov-
ince of science to bestow; it corrects the error of treating the
scientific account as if it were itself metaphysical or religious;
it challenges the tendency to make a religion of science—or a
science of religion—a dogmatic act which destroys the moral dynamic of man. Indeed, many men of science are confronted with
unexpected implications of their own thought and are beginning

to accept, for instance, the trans-spatial and trans-temporal nature of events within spatial matter and within time.

RELIGIOUS PERSPECTIVES attempts to show the fallacy of the apparent irrelevance of God in history. The Series submits that no convincing image of man can arise, in spite of the many ways in which human thought has tried to reach it, without a philosophy of human nature and human freedom which does not exclude God. This image of *Homo cum Deo* implies the highest conceivable freedom, the freedom to step into the very fabric of the universe, a new formula for man's collaboration with the creative process and the only one which is able to protect man from the terror of existence. This image implies further that the mind and conscience are capable of making genuine discriminations and thereby may reconcile the serious tensions between the secular and religious, the profane and sacred. The idea of the sacred lies in what it *is,* timeless existence. By emphasizing timeless existence against reason as a reality, we are liberated, in our communion with the eternal, from the otherwise unbreakable rule of "before and after." Then we are able to admit that all forms, all symbols in religions, by their negation of error and their affirmation of the actuality of truth, make it possible to experience that *knowing* which is above knowledge, and that dynamic passage of the universe to unending unity.

The volumes in this Series will seek to challenge the crisis which separates, to make reasonable a religion that binds and to present the numinous reality within the experience of man. Insofar as the Series succeeds in this quest, it will direct mankind toward a reality that is eternal and away from a preoccupation with that which is illusory and ephemeral.

For man is now confronted with his burden and his greatness: "He calleth to me, Watchman, what of the night? Watchman, what of the night?"[1] Perhaps the anguish in the human soul may be assuaged by the answer, by the *assimilation* of the person in God: "The morning cometh, and also the night: if ye will inquire, inquire ye: return, come."[2]

RUTH NANDA ANSHEN
New York, 1960

[1] Isaiah 21:11.
[2] Isaiah 21:12.

INTERNATIONAL CONFLICT IN THE
TWENTIETH CENTURY
A Christian View

Preface

INTERNATIONAL AFFAIRS IN A DEMOCRACY DO not call for authoritative pronouncements but require the greatest freedom and mobility in the exchange of ideas. The sheer variety of views and approaches is calculated to be useful to the world, provided everybody is not too insistent on having his own way when the decision is finally precipitated. What I have to offer on this subject may represent only the exposition of a personal attitude; and I shall concentrate on the points at which I tend to differ from prevailing views rather than the points on which I imagine myself to be in agreement with them. Perhaps I can hardly help concentrating also on those points on which I find myself continually battering against the frontiers of my own thought.

I am hoping that it may be of some use to have the comments of one who is less preoccupied with "current affairs" as such, and more interested in the processes and patterns of long-term history, in the principles that underlie foreign policy, in the ethical issues involved (particularly as they concern the Christian), and in the role of Christianity during an epoch of global revolution. Our notions about action in the present must depend in part on the feeling that we have about the immediate future: that is to say, about the direction in which we think that the deeper tendencies of history are carrying the world in general. I suspect that I differ from many people on the subject of these deeper processes of time; and, for this reason, I have thought it proper to pay a certain amount of attention to them. But I do not undertake to hold on to any of the ideas which I have put forward, or to cling to them against anything and everything that might be said against them. There are some principles to which we cannot attach ourselves too firmly, and these I should regard as existing in a rare and lofty realm. But, for the rest, the mind can hardly attain the mobility which the case requires. Our greatest danger may come when we turn into hard matters of principle those policies which ought to depend to some degree on time and circumstance.

If we could solve the problem of human relations for external affairs as well as we have solved it for the internal affairs of various nations, the technological development of the world would cause us much less anxiety. All our deadlocks are traceable to difficulties and paradoxes of human relations which have existed for thousands of years. It is urgent that not merely the attention of men who are preoccupied with current affairs, but the best thinking that can be collected from anywhere in the field of the humanities, should be devoted to this great problem.

Two events at the American University, Washington, D.C., provided the occasion for the lectures which are incorporated in the present work. The first was the inauguration of the new School of International Service in October 1958: and the second was the celebration of the transfer of the Wesley Theological Seminary from Westminster, Maryland, to a new campus close to the University. I have to thank the authorities of both these bodies for the honor of their joint invitation and for the pleasure of my visit to them.

H. B.

January, 1960

Introduction

IT IS DANGEROUS TO DISCUSS POLITICS IN A SEP-
arate intellectual realm which is supposed to involve principles
of its own. Under such conditions, certain basic ideas, such as
that of the "state," tend to be puffed up, so that they acquire
the dignity of philosophical concepts and eternal verities. When
we use words like "the state," or "society," or "Germany," it
is safest always to remember that, in the last resort, they represent just so many people. In order to get behind the screen of
conventional political thinking and reach a deeper layer of sin-
cerity inside ourselves, we had better take our start from the
simple picture of a great number of human beings stranded for
a time on this floating globe. Sometimes we allow our abstract
nouns to trick us into cruel paradoxes, and we easily forget
that our collective nouns are dangerous if they are used as more
than a species of shorthand. The Christian does not go hunt-
ing for values in the realm of abstract nouns, because in this
created universe the things that matter are human souls. All
of us ought to live and make our judgments as though, at this
mundane level, nothing but human beings really concerns us,
nothing but human beings really matters, nothing but human
beings really exists.

In any case, so far as the present world is concerned, it is
only human beings that are really relevant when we discuss
problems of morality. The word morality is applicable only to
individual people, only to man in his general human capacity,
or man as he confronts God. Here, again, we have to break
through the screen that distorts the picture when we attach the
term to a mythical entity like "Germany" or an abstract noun

15

like "Communism" or even a collective noun like "the Arabs." Moral responsibility ought to be regarded as a thing which can really be brought home only to individual men and women. When we speak as though there were a separate ethic for the statesman, a peculiar substance called political morality, we are already moving into a world of trick mirrors and optical illusions. The stateman, like the scientist or the poet, will constantly be confronted by the alternative between an act that is more moral and an act that is less moral. But we must not allow that there can be a difference in the quality of the decision in these cases, or a difference in the ethical principles involved. And, certainly for my part, I do not see why in politics even the virtues which I associate with the Christian religion should be suspended for a moment. I mean humility, charity, self-criticism, and acceptance of the problem that Providence sets before one; also, a disposition not to seek to direct affairs as though one had a right to assert a sovereign will in the world—a disposition rather to see that one's action takes the form of a co-operation with Providence.

Because the Christian ethic is closely wrapped up in a doctrine of human relations, it governs the whole intercourse and interplay of human beings. We are not abstracted from its authority when we are engaged, for example, in business deals or in diplomatic affairs. This ethic is one which is animated by a purpose—the earnest Christian always knows that there is something he is wanting to do with the world. He may differ from other people who are wanting to do things with the world, because his objective is bound to be affected by his doctrine of the nature of man, his view of man as a spiritual being. His mundane ends—his absolute values, so far as this world is concerned—are human souls; and if some men prefer to say that the ultimate object is rather the improvement of the human race, his answer would have to be that this object itself is to be achieved by developments in individual people. Perhaps more clearly than anybody else, the Christian has to say that the evolution of mankind must not be through the production of solid uniformity or highly organized monolithic systems. It depends on the development of freedom and differentiation. It involves the diversification of personalities.

We start, therefore, with something like the modern doctrine of individualism; and, on this view, personalities are the only mundane things that matter in the long run. We have to note that there is something irreducible in every human being; but also there is something which cannot be fused into a kind of compound, or merged into a collective mass, or built up into a higher entity that can be more than fictitious. We claim for human beings an expanding freedom and an increasing differentiation. At the same time, we insist that these developments are always accompanied by a growing responsibility.

The modern doctrine of individualism, though it does not seem to please all Christians, emanates from the religious history of our section of the globe. One would not have expected it to emanate from any other quarter; for religion has had tremendous influence on the way in which we stage the whole drama of human life on the earth—the way in which we conceive of the role of human beings under the sun. In the ancient world, the more religion came to be related to the inner man, the more it had the effect of elevating the idea of personality and uncovering the profundities that lie within it. The individual came to be regarded as having something inside himself which overrode the claims of mundane society as such—something so sacred or compelling that it provided the basis for resisting the orders of government and even the tyranny of majorities. As Acton pointed out, it was the human being, not society, which had the soul, the conscience, the inner voice, and the cross reference to eternity. And even the "lapsed Christian," after he has thrown the religious dogmas overboard, carries on for a time with the same world picture, holding fast to the mundane valuations that were associated with it. He attaches himself to the doctrine of individualism, though he may have diminished or diluted the underlying view of man as a spiritual being.

On the general view that I have been describing, men cannot be written off as mere willful bundles of caprice or chance combinations of atoms. And they move to a diversity of ends. From a mundane point of view, the individual has the right to choose the God whom he will worship and the moral end which he will serve. He has the right to make the decisions which are momentous for his inner life—the decision whether to be a Christian or not, for example—though he may be less free in matters which are external, and may not have the right to live in a house that is without drains. Human beings are not to be herded together like cattle, harnessed and organized in a slave system, working for one general purpose which shall be the same for all—a purpose dictated to everybody by a society or a government. Progress is measured, not, for example, by any advance in the exploitation of nature, but by the way in which human personalities are adding to their stature and the inner man is being enriched. Fundamental to this kind of world is respect for the other man's personality, respect for the other man's end—in fact, the ability to put oneself in the other man's place and to see that, if one claims consideration for one's own conscience, the other man may have a conscience too. Furthermore, there is always hope for human beings, though they may seem black in their sins and below the use of reason, so that we are here not to judge the world but to contribute what we can toward saving it. If we are making a peace treaty we are not authorized to ask ourselves: "What punishment of the wrongdoer will best enable us to vindicate righteousness?" Provided we take all the factors into account, we vindicate righteousness when we simply say to ourselves: "What now is the best that we can do for the world?"

1
Morality
and the Way We Stage
the Conflict

POLITICAL ACTION MAY BE ASSESSED ACCORD-
ing to the brilliance of its conception or the degree of its success, but it also has to be measured against the principles of
morality. These are not exhausted in a few famous prohibi-
tions, such as the commandment against stealing. Men who
respect existing rights of property may be pursuing a meaner
form of statesmanship than the social reformer who, because
he subverts such rights, is easily denounced as a thief. Such
people may be keeping the negative commandment while in-
fringing that higher law of charity which has its validity even
in the field of statesmanship. It is always necessary in any case
not to confuse the moral with the moralistic, or to forget that
nations seek to be both judges and parties in the same cause.
We may have the right to condemn actions, and to say, for
example, that religious persecution is always wrong. It is not
equally clear that we have the right to condemn persons or to
imagine that we are better than Mary Tudor merely because
she persecuted and we do not. The Christian in particular cannot claim the right to judge human beings, but may count it
a victory if he persuades the offender that God condemns a
certain course of action. In other words, the cause of morality
is really furthered in so far as an act of self-judgment has been
brought about. The misdeeds of a government which is in a
certain predicament may be angrily condemned by another
government which is committing different crimes at the same
moment and which in fact commits the selfsame crime when
it is in the same predicament. In these various ways, the crudi-
ties of popular ethics render the political exploitation of morality a comparatively easy matter. By making consistent use of
methods that were developed in the West—by turning the
weapons of democracy against democracy itself—the Com-

munists have brought to a climax the use of moral indignation as a weapon of power politics.

The conflicts of the present day have made it clear that one of the greatest hurdles which the human spirit has to surmount is a lack of imagination due to a stiff-necked form of righteousness. Behind many of our present-day differences of opinion in the political realm there is in fact a concealed conflict on a point of ethics; and for the sake of clarity, it is important that this should be brought out into the light of day. It would seem that Christians ought to feel themselves under a particular obligation to take part in this conflict. They may be missing opportunities if they assume too easily that their morality is identical with that of the political world in general.

The ethical conflict in question would seem to have its parallel in one which is recorded in the Gospels—the conflict conducted by the Lord not against the publicans and sinners but against the Pharisees, those upright people who are presented to us as the most priggish moralizers of their day. Here, at the very heart of Christian teaching and Christian narrative, we see a Christ who is reproved for consorting with the disreputable, and who stands in high combat with the righteousness of the stiff-necked. He does not pass judgment on the superficial act, but proportions praise and blame to men's opportunities, to the materials they had to work on, and to the degree of temptation and test to which they were exposed. He calls men to constant self-criticism, and shows the Pharisee that what he imagined to be his virtue might owe more to good fortune than he had ever realized. The very names of Tyre and Sidon seemed to be a symbol of pagan sin; but to the more respectable cities of his own day, Christ says that if Tyre and Sidon had seen the mighty works that they had seen—if Tyre and Sidon had had the Son of God in their midst—they would have been better than modern Capernaum, and would have repented in sackcloth and ashes. It is as though Christ were to say to Britain and America: "Don't pride yourselves on being better than the Germans were. If the Germans had been as fortunate as you have been, and if they had been in the same position, they might have behaved at least as virtuously as you."

In all fields except the field of interstate relations, the world has made a great advance because it has been prepared to follow these principles. We do not burn witches now—we ask the psychoanalyst to cure them. If adolescent crime increases we may not exonerate the culprits, but we do enquire about the conditions which have caused the generalization of the evil. If human conduct requires to be improved, the policeman, the judge, the confessor and the prophet may address themselves to the responsibility of individuals. But we achieve something, too, if we apply ourselves to external conditions, as when we abolish slums, establish educational systems, or put guardians at the doors of our picture galleries. The essential nature of man may not be altered, but human behavior in general is sometimes improved, by the establishment of an order of things which has the effect of reducing the temptation. The principle may even be applied to the case of aggression in international affairs; for even in the international world a sort of stability is possible in which the rulers of great states cease to think of the world as being open to large-scale conquest. There is a sense in which it is not the statesman's business (as it might be the business of a religious revivalist) to improve human nature at its core; and a statesman is weak if he relies too much on exhortation or says that he could have dealt with his problems if only human nature somewhere had been better than it is. It is a statesman's business to know human beings as they really are and to deal with them as such. If he establishes a tax which leads to smuggling where previously there had been no smuggling, he cannot excuse himself by throwing all the blame on men whom he has tempted too far. In fact, therefore, it is the statesman most of all who has to adopt the attitude that I have described, and avoid the faults of the Pharisee. And this maxim applies to a supreme degree in international affairs. When Sir John Simon became Foreign Secretary in London, I remember being told that in England there was a prejudice against having a lawyer in that position. The legal mind is liable to be too rigid in the acts of judgment required.

The point can be illustrated by a nineteenth-century example. When Gladstone was preparing for disestablishment in Ireland, Queen Victoria sought to deter him by drawing his attention to the agrarian outrages in that country. In her opinion, they called simply for condemnation and punishment; and certainly they were things which one would expect a religious confessor to reprove, the police to repress, and the courts of justice to condemn. Gladstone replied, however, that the government was not surprised to see the outrages, and that these things were rather to be expected, human nature being what it is. This particular kind of crime in Ireland, he said, had something of the nature of a disease. The government was proposing to remedy the conditions which had helped to produce it, though it realized that the remedy was not one that could come very quickly into effect. Curiously enough, though the peasants were the sinners in these outrages and the landlords were the victims, the act of statesmanship had to be directed in the long run against the latter. To judge from this, the peasants were not so much to blame for their acts of violence as the landlords were for the position they held—a position which, however legal, had the effect of goading men into crime.

In the twentieth century we are sometimes content to condemn rebellions and acts of violence when they are directed against ourselves or against our allies. But when they are directed against our enemies we fix our eyes on the conditions which provoked the tumult, and we sympathize with the insurgents, condemning even the police measures which are taken against them. Here is a wide field in which we can be as arbitrary as we like, because nobody can compel us to make our thinking at one moment square with our thinking at another moment. The Whig historians used to take the line that, since tyranny pays little regard to reasonable entreaty and to merely verbal protests, the only way in which people can show their discontent—the only way in which they can convince the world that something is hurting them—is by a desperate resort to violence. It was an old maxim of statesmanship that some of the responsibility for such acts of violence attaches to those who rigidly defend the existing *status quo,* particularly if they have left the victims without any other means of redress. In the international world as well as in the internal affairs of our own country, we may be partly responsible for other people's sins.

Certain Irishmen, who once saw cruel things happening close at hand, have never throughout their lives forgiven Mr. de Valera for his conduct between thirty and forty years ago. There have been other people, however, who, having observed his career in more recent decades, have wondered how such a man could ever have been condemned to death as a criminal. It would seem that, in politics, the act of judgment can be astonishingly easy—and the verdict can seem appallingly self-evident—provided a small number of discrepant facts or inconvenient considerations are kept out of sight. The real wisdom of a political decision, therefore, often depends (amongst other things) upon the catholicity with which all the factors in the case are allowed for, and all the relevant considerations embraced. It is dangerous to imagine that ours is a world in which masses of men on the one side have freely opted for wickedness, while on the other side there is a completely righteous party, whose virtue is superior to conditioning circumstances.

The reasons for suspecting such a diagram of the situation are greatly multiplied if the ethical judgment is entangled with a political one—if, for example, the wickedness is charged against a rival political party, or imputed to another nation just at the moment when, for reasons of power politics, that nation is due to stand as the potential enemy in any case. There is no realm of life which calls for profounder rethinking than that of international affairs—no realm where it is more necessary for us to do hard things with our personalities, unloading ourselves of former prejudices and piercing through successive layers of insincerity. Even in time of war, when passions can hardly be kept from rising high, all sanity depends on our keeping, deep at the bottom of everything, some remembrance of that humanity which we have in common with our bitterest enemies. It may be a prejudice of mine, but I wonder whether Christians, if they could disentangle their minds from the conventional mundane systems that constrict them, might not within a decade contribute something creative to this deeper cause of human understanding.

A great part of the globe is now in a position somewhat analogous to that of the Irish peasantry about which Gladstone and Queen Victoria had their differences nearly a century ago. It has resorted to various degrees of rebellion against what is regarded as Western imperialism or Western exploitation or Western ascendancy. Such a revolt was a thing which had long been predicted; and if we resent it too much, this is perhaps because we have not sufficiently given ourselves to the task of imagining what our feelings would have been if we had been born Arabs or Indians. When nothing is done to meet the demands of such peoples—and even if their aspirations are thwarted by international law or by the machinery of the United Nations—the forces at the bottom of these volcanoes will throw up unscrupulous leaders, desperate and ambitious men, willing to resort to intrigue and violence. Within fifty years or so, another aspect of this world conflict is likely to emerge, for terrible trouble is going to fall upon the white man from the vast colored world of Africa. We can be sure that, when the moment arrives, this African volcano will throw up its desperate, ruthless leaders, as generally happens in such cases. And once again, we shall hoax ourselves with the delusion that the crisis is a fictitious one—that all the trouble is really due to the operation of this handful of wicked men. We had better examine our own sins; for, if we hold powers and privileges in the territory of such peoples by virtue of treaties concluded when they knew no better, or when they were taken at a disadvantage, or when they were in no position to resist us, we are like the landlords in Gladstone's Ireland—our legalistic rights may be more reprehensible than the violence they so naturally provoke. In the *Review of Politics* for October 1957, Professor Fitzsimons quotes some moving remarks by Mr. Abdulgani, the representative of Indonesia at the first Suez Conference in London in August, 1956:

> Most of the treaties which are a reflection of international law do not respect the sanctity of men as equal human beings irrespective of their race, or their creed or locality. Most of the existing laws between Asian and African countries and the old-established western world are more or less outmoded and should be regarded as a burden of modern life. They should be revised and made more adaptable to modern national relations and the emancipation of all parts of mankind. . . . This process of emancipation is sometimes carried out gracefully . . . sometimes it creates explosive repercussions. . . . But nobody can defy the process of this emancipation which is the inevitable course in human history.

While today the Western bloc and the Eastern bloc confront

one another, a considerable section of the globe stands uncommitted to either. The very regions which in the last resort would fear Russian predominance the most, and would find Russian power directly on top of them, are the most responsible for some of our present difficulties. They take action against us not because they dread us the more but because at the moment we present them with their more immediate problem. Also they want to take their opportunity while the greater powers of the world are so occupied with one another. Russia supports them in their anti-imperialist policies, and here she is in the happy position that the democracies once held, for the path of virtue happens to coincide with that of her own self-interest. Russia makes a profit if she does no more than succeed in dislodging us from the various types of position that we hold in Asia and Africa. She has it within her power to see that this so-called "imperialist" problem shall be the presiding issue in international affairs for a long time. We cannot deny that the issue exists if the people most concerned—and indeed the uncommitted part of the world—are insistent that, to them, this is the most momentous matter of all. The opinion—whether right or wrong—of that whole area is in any case going to be important in the future. It can make a real difference now, and can override the effects of our colossal power, as we have had to realize in the case of the Arab countries. Precisely because a major war is too terrible a thing to undertake for an ambiguous cause, or upon a side issue, moral factors are becoming more important than before in respect of intermediate or peripheral problems. In those cases the resort to nuclear weapons would be too dreadful to contemplate, and even colossal power has to take more account of world opinion than used to be the case.

In 1919 the victor powers established an international system which forbade all "aggression" in future and prohibited the further acquisition of empire in the manner hitherto prevailing. It left existing empires intact, and even guaranteed their existence, since any offensive against them could now be condemned as an act of aggression. The League of Nations itself was not even to intervene between Britain and her Indian subjects, the relations of these latter being regarded as an internal affair. Empire could now be retained more cheaply than ever before in history; for on these terms it was guaranteed even after it had ceased to have any correlation with power. In reality, a great many of our troubles since 1919 have been caused by the fact that we have devised no satisfactory machinery for the peaceful revision of the *status quo*. The new machinery tended to freeze this more definitely than the old had been able to do. Treaties themselves may be unfair or unjust—or they may become so through the passage of time. But where the power which profits by the unjustice possesses a *liberum veto,* so that it can block any revision, there is great difficulty in securing a satisfactory arrangement. Because there has been a tendency to take refuge in legalism, it would seem that those who desire revision can always be made to appear as aggressors. In some ways it has been more difficult to adjust the territorial and treaty arrangements of the world to either the power situation or the rights of the case than in the period before 1914.

In so far as the so-called imperialism of the Western powers is in question, it is possible for us to have the law on our side while the ethics of the case are against us. In normal times, it may be sufficient to have the law on our side because the law has the authentic consent of the world; but the situation is different in an age of rapid transition and overturn, when issues have to be submitted to the ultimate ethical test. Those who defend the *status quo* may claim that they are not attacking anybody, but we know that they may be exercising (as foreigners) some species of domination over other people who resent that domination, however legal it may be. Those who defend the *status quo* may, indeed, not be attacking anybody, but even they only hold their advantages by virtue of the exercise of latent power; and, as in the case of the French in Algeria, a rebellion may bring that force into overt use. It is a question whether one can clear the world of the most unsatisfactory features of power politics at the present day, while one goes on enjoying (against the wishes of the people concerned) the benefits that one acquired in the power politics of past centuries. Those who attack the *status quo* are guilty in the sense that they resort to violence; but if, for example, they are seeking to free people who desire to be freed, we have to remember that, without such illegal violence against the *status quo*, liberty could not have come to the world either in the age of George III or in the age that followed Metternich. In a stable world we might be able to be legalistic, but in an age of revolution, when new peoples are awakening to political consciousness, the culpability of the power that attacks the *status quo* cannot be discussed in entire isolation from the question of the justice of the revisionist demands. It is still the case that, until some act of violence occurs, we do not realize that there is a problem to be solved, do not see that there is any need to have a negotiation at all, do not believe that there are victims demanding some kind of redress. Before a wrong can be righted it is still necessary to override the *liberum veto* of the power that profits from the unfairness of the situation; and the victims are not going to lie quiet when, in a new world order, they find that they have the power as well as the justice on their side. In the imperfect state of our own international order, it is clear that it requires an act of violence to secure that a topic is in any effective sense put on the agenda at all. There is even a pitfall when we tell the world that we are ready to negotiate; for those who have the advantage of the *status quo* still possess the *liberum veto,* and they may not concede anything in negotiation unless they are threatened with further violence or confronted by a signal action which mobilizes world opinion. Under such a system, the role of force is not merely to further the aggressor in the sense that we usually give to that word. And in any case force is maintaining our own system all the time; latent force is maintaining injustice on occasion. Force is needed to jerk our attention (or the attention of the world) to the need for a change in the *status quo*.

If, therefore, the Western powers have had to retreat after a violent demonstration or before the threat of violence, we ought not to regard this as necessarily a reverse or a cause of shame. It is rather a proof that, once we have been stung to attention, we are ready to listen to justice or make a concession to reasonableness. Too often, however, we treat these things as reverses; and in consequence of this, when we have given way to justice, the world sometimes thinks that we have given way to fear. In all this, we are allowing ourselves to be caught on the wrong foot, for it would have been better if we had anticipated the act of violence (as our wiser statesmen have sometimes done) so that we clearly held the initiative. The time for us to resolve to defend the *status quo* was in the First World War, when such a policy would have had the effect of minimizing the consequences of war and would have amounted to the decision to reduce the role of war in history. It was we ourselves who loosened the soil and shook the basis of mere legalism and historical rights, opening the way for that flood of uncontrollable change which would make all frontiers doubtful and bring all imperial systems into question. There is no refuge for us now but to be more eager than the Russians to see the authentic development of liberty in the world, more ready than the Communists to bring about changes in the existing system.

The conflict between East and West embraces several momentous issues, but it arises firstly out of the new situations created by the power of Russia. During the eighteenth and nineteenth centuries our predecessors were repeatedly haunted by the vision of the menace which, even under the Czarist regime, they thought was bound to come if ever the great Russian Bear really stirred itself and collected its power. I think that only in the twentieth century did there come to prevail that kind of naïveté which expected Russia to be nonaggressive when her accumulated power had given her the predominance. And, because of that naïveté, Russia emerges to full stature under conditions that are particularly disadvantageous for the West. In reality, throughout modern history, Spain, France, Germany and Russia have been the aggressors in turn, as they came into parallel positions that gave them the opening for this. I do not see how anybody could claim that even the British Empire was built up without a similar kind of aggrandizement; nor, even in the twentieth century, have small states themselves failed to reveal the same acquisitive tendencies when they had the same kind of local opportunity. It is a pity that, in this respect, the Russians have proved to be so like the rest of human nature, so like what the Czardom was expected to become if ever it had the chance.

The actions of human beings, then, are not unrelated to conditions, and the generalized conduct of a great aggregate of men will be more closely influenced by situation and predicament than the behavior of a particular individual. The general posture of a government, and the role adopted by a given state in a given period, will be affected to a surprising degree by various types of necessity, and by the temptations which a particular conjuncture may offer. It may even be true that, human nature being what it is, the various nations become aggressors in turn as the changing state of the world brings its temptations and opportunities. If a naval empire is less inimical to freedom than any other kind of empire, this very fact may also be explicable to a considerable degree in terms of forces and conditions. Situations and circumstances have their part in the explanation of the fact that a given nation at one moment leads the resistance against aggression and at another moment becomes an aggressor itself. If it appears that a career of aggression is closely associated with the character of a particular person, it is still true that situations and circumstances may have had their part in the evolution of such a man or in his climb to national leadership. To a considerable degree, conditions decide that at a given moment one nation may be rebelling against the existing order while another stands as the defender of the *status quo*. It even happens that certain conditions in the international world make for moderation in politics, and there are times when an aggressor thinks himself very daring if he contemplates no more than a minor territorial acquisition. Personalities make a difference, for men are not the mere slaves of conditions; and partly personalities (but partly, perhaps, even here, conditions once again) may decide that aggression or rebellion or the defence of the *status quo* is conducted with a certain degree of generosity or chivalry or moderation. But it would seem to take more virtue than many of us realize—a virtue almost superior to conditioning circumstances—to keep a country at peace when the situation is one which offers temptations and opportunities to a potential aggressor. And the situation itself may bring about the downfall of the man who in such circumstances insists on peace, so that a more violent leader rises to the seat of power. A wise and moderate statesman may make the path of self-interest coincide with the path of virtue, so that, for example, his career of aggression comes to be identified with a great human cause. A creative and audacious statesman, commanding an empire that has been put on the defensive, might trump the aces of his enemies by a liberating movement that made him the initiator of a new era of change, though conditions had seemed to prescribe the mere preservation of the *status quo*. When we contemplate the misfortunes of the former Hapsburg territories in Central Europe since the First World War, we must wonder whether a bolder and more imaginative policy in the face of the rising forces of the nineteenth century might not have enabled the Hapsburg Empire to go on fulfilling its European function without affronting the ideas and ideals of a new era. When we contemplate the history of the British Empire in the nineteenth century, we can see how an obscurantist and rigid policy could have brought Great Britain to disaster and robbed the world of the Commonwealth of Nations.

Apart from any danger that he might fear from the power of Russia, Hitler declared that Communism as such was the international enemy, but the democracies then refused to adopt this attitude. Hostility to Communism became the basis of their foreign policy only after Russia herself (and, later, China) had become so formidable—only after the revolutionary cause had come to be linked with colossal power. It is important to be discriminating about these matters and to know whether the key to one's foreign policy is opposition to a great power or opposition to a doctrinal system. The West may be mistaken, and may be unnecessarily weakening itself, if it takes its stand against egalitarian ideals as such, or even gives the appearance of doing so. If it merely tries to hold the dykes against revolution all over the world, all revolutionized states will be thrown into the arms of Russia, even where power politics would have drawn them apart. The missionary zeal of Communism provides added momentum and additional weapons to aggression, but democracy did the same in the era of French Revolutionary conquest; and still it might not have been wise to say that "democracy" as such was the enemy. If we say that Communism is oppressive, there was a time when democracy was condemned because it was associated with the French Revolutionary "Terror" and the Jacobin dictatorship. The tyranny may have an organic relationship, not with the egalitarian ideal as such, but with revolution of any sort, since even liberal revolutions—and even those that are associated with Christianity—move in a relentless manner toward despotism, and terrible crimes may be committed by men who are anxious to transform the whole order of things in a hurry. The chief danger of a policy which makes Communism the primary enemy is the fact that one is easily seduced into thinking that it is sufficient to hold the *status quo* against revolution or social change, and against the missionary zeal of impatient reformers. One may even come to think it a virtue to preserve abusive and quasi-feudal systems against the archenemy, against the reforming ardor of Communism. For this reason it is hazardous to oppose a missionary ideal except by confronting it with another that is equally optimistic and zealous.

There does actually exist a conflict of ideals between Western Democracy and Eastern Communism. It is now centered on the undeveloped and uncommitted sections of the globe, and it will be both the policy and the interest of Soviet Russia to keep it there. It is a conflict in which we might imaginably be defeated by measures that always come short of actual war —measures which might leave us with colossal weapons on our hands, and never an opportunity of using them. While we are all braced for one kind of war, and piling up our massive armaments for it, the situation has been changing, and we must take care not to be caught out by a different kind of conflict that now fills the stage—the conflict of ideals. If we resent the missionary zeal of Communism, this is perhaps partly because the new conjuncture finds us without the same sense of mission. If we lack this zeal, the new conflict will find us the mere prisoners of conditioning circumstances—the desperate defenders of a *status quo* that is crumbling beneath our feet. In the new situation, moral factors are going to play a more important part than we sometimes recognize, and we possess the moral assets if only we were not too preoccupied with war, and perhaps too generally afraid, to use them. Perhaps we ought to ask ourselves whether, even from the point of view of *Realpolitik,* we have not been wrong in those cases where we have been afraid to put our ideals of liberty into fairly consistent practice in the unsettled areas of the globe.

2

The Scientific Method in the Realm of Politics

IN 1939, ENGLISHMEN OFTEN TOLD THEMSELVES
that they must take care not to repeat the particular mistake
they had made in July 1914. In this they were making a primitive kind of analogy between two situations, and a hit-or-miss
decision about what went wrong in 1914. At the time of the
Peace Conference of 1919, some people insisted on the necessity of avoiding the mistakes that had been made at the Congress of Vienna. All this merely had the effect of confirming
the obsession which the twentieth-century peacemakers already
had for the principle of nationality. Now we try to discover why
the old Treaty of Vienna succeeded so much better than the
Treaty of Versailles. Sir Anthony Eden convinced us, I think,
that he had built up his image of Colonel Nasser on the feeling that here was a recurrence of the pattern provided by Hitler. And similarly, when we say that we will have no "appease-
ment," we clutch at a rough analogy and base our argument
on a nickname, bringing to momentous issues a wilder im-
petuosity of thought than would be permitted to a schoolboy
mending a bicycle.

We might conclude that when people think about general
policy they have nothing but history and experience from
which to draw a certain amount of enlightenment. They may
be primitive and unmethodical in the use of these materials,
however; and when it is suggested that they might become
more scientific, we need not behave as though we were still in
the Dark Ages, terrified of the advance of this malevolent thing
called science. Those whose acceptance of the idea is blocked
by rigid notions about Victorian physics easily overlook the
primitive and haphazard nature of the present alternative. As
things stand at the moment, one can smuggle into a political
argument all kinds of generalizations, formulas, nicknames and

41

analogies which answer to men's wishful thinking; and these come into currency without having to be submitted to any very methodical kind of test. In one age democrats are saying that only kings are responsible for wars, but in another age they say that it is the Communist revolutionaries. In one mood they see some of the natives of Algeria fighting for freedom and self-determination; in another mood they see them as wicked men trying to change the legal *status quo* by violence. Sometimes the world is content to clutch at a wild thesis, such as the old cliché that the armament makers are responsible for wars; and it does not always remember how much methodical thinking one would bring to the discussion of parallel relationships between inanimate objects, such as the causes of weakness in a machine. We might enquire whether there is not at least a foothold for more systematic thinking in this field—whether there is not in fact a gleam of something that might have potentialities for the future.

The examples that have been mentioned show that at least people do make correlations—or clutch at something of the sort—between events that occur in their political memory or the things that they learn in history. Those who speak of the uniqueness of historical events, as though no correspondences or connections or meaningful relationships could exist between them, are repudiating some of the most interesting things that historical thought itself has ever achieved. They are in fact rejecting one of the essential ideas put forward by Ranke, when he established history on a more scientific basis. We could not speak of a statesman as having experience if it were not possible for a man to carry forward, from the successive episodes of his political career, a certain deposit, calculated to be useful to him at the next conjuncture, strange (and even unique) though that conjuncture might be. This deposit might hardly exist in the form of hard information, but might have refined itself into a statesman's "touch" or a statesmanlike "feeling" for things—an extra sensibility which can go on existing after a man has forgotten the successive layers of knowledge on which it had originally been based. It could only emerge if the man concerned had made intelligent correlations between the various parts of his knowledge—the various events of his life— churning them into a form of wisdom, transmuting them into "experience." In a similar way, a man who had once made a study of the past might go on reaping benefit from this after he had forgotten all the historical facts he had ever assimilated. Without this ability to fuse our knowledge into our experience, we might learn the events of Henry VII's reign, and retain them in our memory, yet bring to the present day only a deadly literal-mindedness and an inability to keep pace with the fluidity of events.

If wisdom and experience ultimately depend on correlations which are made between events, it is a question whether people in the twentieth century are as methodical and resourceful in this matter as their predecessors in the eighteenth and nineteenth centuries. One gets the impression that the men in our government departments, oppressed by the amount of typescript they have to read, lack the time and the kind of mental liberation that would enable them to reign at ease in their own realm. They can hardly stop to reflect on history and experience, to diagnose long-term tendencies in the world, to think about the process of things in time, and to meditate on the relationship between events. It is possibly true that the history written two or three generations ago, though so much less satisfactory from an academic point of view, was a better training in statesmanship and human wisdom than the kind of work which is commonly produced at the present day. Some of us have doubts about the great scheme which is embodied in Professor Toynbee's *Study of History,* and the experts sometimes tell us that the amazing range of this writer's scholarship is counterbalanced by its faults and inaccuracies. Strewn in his works, however, are many profound historical insights, springing from an imaginative use of quasi-scientific processes; and though the methods can be traced back for two centuries (or to antiquity) and may be limited in their value even now, they do at least point to interesting possibilities in the future. It is too often forgotten that in politics, as in economics, there is no way of increasing wisdom except by thinking more methodically—though certainly not with less imagination—on all that history and experience can offer. Those of us who like to stress the uniqueness of every historical event or conjuncture or situation or episode can sometimes agree that these unique phenomena are really compounds, each of them standing alone in the sense that it is an unprecedented combination, but each of them reducible to elements that are recurrent and classifiable. I do not think that historians themselves are uninterested in attempts that have been made at stimulating forms of correlation—the attempt of one scholar, for example, to show how many of the well-known figures of the Romantic movement had been products of the manse. I should like to see this enchanting technique of methodical collation applied to everything possible—falling in love, conversions to Roman Catholicism, national aggression, atrocities in war, and the incidence of the appreciation of Wordsworth's poetry.

The attempt to develop this kind of thinking to a higher power has proceeded far in economics and sociology, but it has long been checked in the realm of politics and international affairs. The obstruction seems to have been caused partly, as we have seen, by dubious inferences from the uniqueness of historical events, but also by an anxiety to do justice to human freedom and responsibility. It seems to be assumed that because the free choices of human beings introduce a chancy and unpredictable factor into history, scientific methods of any conceivable kind must be inapplicable, and no sector of the field can be reduced to order. Without asserting that a form of science is attainable, we ought to ask whether some of the arguments against the possibility of such a thing are not themselves somewhat deceptive. It may help to remove an obstruction, therefore, if we look once again at the texture of history.

If we take one side of the picture, we see human beings as responsible for their actions, as sovereign within a certain area of choice, and (to that degree) as makers of their own history. The present generation is perhaps in danger of underestimating the subtlety and the complexity of the historical process, and particularly the play of personality and the role of contingency in human events. Every moment in history presents unique combinations of circumstance, and some small and apparently irrelevant occurrence may assume unexpected importance because it happens to be pivotal. For this reason we can never really foresee the turns that history in general may take, and we ought not to be unreasonably depressed by the nightmare predictions that people so often like to produce about the developments of the remote future. There is a considerable worldly wisdom in the religious precept which reminds us that it is possible to take too much thought for the morrow. Because great things may turn on a tiny pivot, the resolution of an individual human being sometimes acquires a magnified importance in the world. The process of history may even give extraordinary leverage at a certain moment to the decisions or the initiative of some single person. We can all remember occasions on which our doing a trifle more or a trifle less than our duty has had a magnified effect, which could never have been calculated in advance. Furthermore, the role of the individual will is all the more important in that history is a field in which big decisions sometimes seem to be carried by narrow margins.

It would appear that even in the twentieth century a world war may be won or lost almost by a hairbreadth. A comparatively small number of people might decide the balance between a permanently conservative and permanently socialist England. I wonder whether it was not a comparatively small number of important people who had the effect of making it appear to us that the ancient Jews were religious while the ancient Greeks were rather scientific. After the Bolshevik revolution of 1917, one cannot help feeling that in recent times (as in the days of the ancient Roman Empire) a mere handful of men, provided they have faith and a sense of mission, can produce an extraordinary landslide in history within a very short period of time.

It would be wrong to imagine that the individual is free of his responsibility—or that his will is unimportant—even when he is a single member of a vast crowd. Thomas Carlyle was right when, in discussing the responsibility for the condition of France on the eve of the Revolution, he blamed every man in the country who had done less than his duty—every man, he said, whether "Shoeblack" or "Sovereign Lord." One of the difficulties of modern democracy lies in the fact that individuals do not matter less than they used to do, but they tend to think that they matter less—they imagine that the responsibility loses itself because it is so dispersed. One can do less than one's duty while nursing the hope that everybody else will behave better, so that the small delinquency will not build itself up into a colossal evil. One may say to oneself that here is a particular liberty that everybody else will be taking: how can one be expected to swim against the tide? Carlyle's thesis carries the consequence that wars may be caused, or empires fall, or civilizations decline, not necessarily through some extraordinary criminality in the first place, but from multitudinous cases of petty betrayal or individual neglect. Even when we see what

appears to be a colossal impersonal crime—like the coming of
the Nazis to power in Germany—we have only to stare at the
picture a little while, and we soon realize that, behind the
shocking event at the center, the blame goes back to the vast
numbers of individuals, each guilty of small derelictions of duty
or petty compliances with vested interests. Every one of these
individuals may be astoundingly unaware of the importance
of the decisions he is taking, whether in the business realm or
the journalistic field or the voting booth. Sometimes it is a multitude of little local egotisms, and little pressures on the part
of vested interests, which drive politicians into a corner and
then lead to a deplorable act of aggression by a government. It
is conceivable that it would have required no great change in
human nature generally, but only a little less willfulness in great
numbers of people at one time and another, to prevent the war
of 1914, or to hold in check some of the great evils of the
twentieth century. There would be no point in our discussing
international affairs at this moment if important things did not
depend on our individual acts of volition.

But, though men help to make their history by the decisions
they take, there is a sense in which they are victims of events—
caught up in a time process which they only partly understand.
They are born at a certain date and place, and in a certain
station; and there are parts of their very selves which have been
affected or influenced by previous events. In any case, human
beings are not always vindicating their freedom and autonomy
in magnificent acts of volition; and some of the defects of human nature become apparent when we see the degree to which
man's virtue and respectability are subject to conditioning circumstances. Even subtle changes in society are calculated to
have a curious influence upon the conduct of human beings.
An English businessman said some time ago that the complexi-
ties of modern regulations and the delays caused by red tape

had had such disastrous effects on his enterprises that, in order to cut his way through them, he had been driven to resort to practices which during the whole of his previous life he would have regarded as immoral.

More cataclysmic upheavals in our general environment tend to have a still more radical effect on human behavior. Men who for decades have pursued a respectable course in a well-ordered society may be transformed into brutes during the terrors and cutthroat struggles of a revolution. When one set of people is in this kind of predicament, nobody can say that the men concerned are right for so submitting to the force of circumstances; but such offenses can easily be condemned out of hand by other people who (though they do not know it) would behave in the same way if they were in the same predicament —people who are lucky, therefore, because their virtue is not put to the same test. In international politics, as we have seen, it is easier for some governments to be virtuous than for others, because the course of virtue happens to coincide with the requirements of self-interest. Powers which have a general concern for the defence of the existing *status quo,* for example, find it comparatively easy to be peaceloving, and to seek a combination against aggressors, at any rate until the situation has become desperate. Certainly, the Hapsburgs of Austria, threatened by new forces that had arisen in the world, and faced by the eventual loss of their empire, chose in 1914 not to go under without fighting. It would be interesting to know whether any empire that is in retreat before rising forces in society ever consents to make the last crucial sacrifices and to go under without fighting, if it sees a chance of saving these things by a resort to war.

There are, then, two aspects of the historical realm. On the one hand, I can feel sure that the war of 1914 might have been avoided if only one or two people had made slightly different decisions which I think it was open to them to make. On the other hand, I should still regard it as important to relate even those decisions to conditioning circumstances, such as the constitution of Germany, the state of the Hapsburg Empire, and the desperate tension then existing in Europe. In any case, the catastrophe of 1914 has to be examined in the light of historical processes which are traceable to a date forty or a hundred years earlier than the occurrence of the crisis itself. Political action is hardly likely to be wise if it is conducted without some knowledge of those historical processes, or some sense of their existence.

Sometimes a moralistic prejudice obstructs our recognition of the things in human nature which for practical purposes can be regarded as constant. Though all men are free to make their own choice in the matter, a statesman can in fact say that, "human nature being what it is," such and such a piece of political highhandedness is likely to provoke people to an act of violence. Without this degree of predictability in events it is difficult to imagine how an art of statesmanship could come into existence at all. The statesman may commit the piece of highhandedness in question, and, to be sure, at the next stage in the story, he can turn his moral indignation upon the acts of violence which he has provoked and which he ought to have foreseen. In such a case, there is higher morality in being less moralistic, and policy is one degree better when, somewhere in the background, there has been a little science.

The odds and ends of generalizations and maxims, analyses and correlations, which are now available for students of policy by no means constitute what we could call a science. I imagine that a good deal of advance has been made in the structural analysis of historical situations, however, such as that which underlies the predicament of contemporary France. In fact, maxims of government, even maxims of foreign policy, go back to the days of antiquity, and interesting things (different from the current conclusions of common sense) have been produced in certain areas of the subject. We ought therefore to enquire whether it is an absolute obstruction (and not merely some controllable error on our part) that has prevented the study of human relations from developing as wonderfully as the study of inanimate things. The democracies of the twentieth century would appear to have lost something of what their predecessors possessed, and this seems chiefly to be due to the fact that they find it more easy to behave merely moralistically when they are taken by surprise. They lost for a time—though perhaps they are relearning after bitter experience—some of that ancient understanding of the balance of power as a system which enabled small states to preserve their existence and to have a real part (not merely the role of satellites) in international affairs. The flouting of certain well-known maxims has in fact produced the disastrous results which some of our predecessors had learned to anticipate. That a radical change of long-accepted frontiers will provoke the demand for more change and counterchange, bringing about a general instability of frontiers; that developments inside single countries can change the distribution of power in the world, and then, if no machinery exists for the peaceful alteration of the *status quo,* the resort to violence can be regarded as virtually inevitable; that, unless confined to limited purposes, war will raise more devils and unpredictable horrors than your own victory in the conflict will ever put down—these are ancient theses, and the total submergence of them during the First World War has amounted to what, in international affairs, must count as a decline of civilization. In the nineteenth century one even meets with the prediction that the danger in future democracy would lie in the moralistic willfulness and the scorn of more scientific procedures both of which have already proved a misfortune in foreign policy.

Since human conduct is so often affected by the pressure of conditioning circumstances, we can learn to a certain degree how to deal with it. There is a sufficient constancy in human nature to make it useful to study the operation of external influences, useful also to consider the activity of human beings in the mass. Napoleon and Hitler, Mussolini and Stalin, may differ greatly from one another, and their action at a given moment may be unpredictable, but still we can analyze the operation of power politics, we can set out to make a systematic study of power. At what might almost be called the birth of modern science, Francis Bacon advised the students of his day to turn their attention to certain kinds of phenomena which, because they were so familiar, were accepted as obvious, when in reality they needed to be re-examined. He instanced a number of things which were not material objects at all: such things as heat, density, gravity, and the rotation of the heavenly bodies. In the realm of human affairs there are parallel phenomena which we tend to go on accepting in their obvious form and with traditional prejudices; and the student, whether of history or of politics, might find it useful to re-examine them as scientifically as possible. Amongst them would be aggression, the balance of power, wartime atrocities, the role of force in diplomatic affairs, the notion of "the war for righteousness," and the conception of an international order.

The eighteenth century could produce general theses about the balance of power, formulating the conditions under which small states can have independent play and perform a genuine role in international affairs. Professor Toynbee can tell us how the balance of power in a given system tends to shift from the center to the periphery; how the existence of such a balance tends to keep the average level of power comparatively low;

and how useful it is to have an independent state, holding the balance between the greater ones, and retaining its own freedom of action. Everything is not subject to mere chance or human caprice, and there is still an opening for a methodical treatment of events, actions, tendencies and processes—for an analysis of the more constant factors in a situation, and a measurement of the area within which human choices can effectively operate. The student of history may lack some of the principal constituents of the man of action; but it is perhaps the case that the man of action has made mistakes for lack of a long-term view of the structure of the Arab world, the present stage of its historical development, and the operation of historical forces there.

Fifty years ago history and natural science confronted one another as fair competitors—almost (one might say) as equal powers. If scientific thinking has marched ahead of historical thinking in the meantime—if our control over nature has outrun any science of human relations which we possess—I wonder whether this is not because of the intellectual audacity with which the scientists confronted (instead of evading) the paradoxes that kept arising. The natural scientists have moved into subtle realms, and the term "science" must be taken with flexibility and imagination, not excluding the possibility that physics is an art as well as a science. We might use the term without superstition, and chiefly to suggest the development of more methodical thinking, the readiness to pursue problems beyond the realm of rough common sense, and the determination not to be excluded by moralistic prejudices from the analysis of anything. I am not sure, however, that we might not even stretch our minds to imagine a "science" which, while dominating a vast area of its subject (namely, the political conduct of men) knew that it still had to travel, so to speak, with one or more unknown quantities. The results of such a science would not by any means be useless, though they would need to be handled with great elasticity of mind. The man who sought to take advantage from them would have to be like Napoleon, with alternative plans of battle, waiting to see which of the possible courses the enemy would choose, and then pressing the required button. There is point in discovering what I shall call "laws" even when these are true only in a conditional sense —true, for example, with the provision "other things being equal." It is something to be able to discern such laws even if they are valid only as representing a tendency or a bias in events—a factor which the wise politician will therefore want to take into account. There may be generalizations about people in the mass, even though, when one comes to points of detail, every individual in the mass has his own peculiarities. Exceptions might occur, and yet these might not affect the validity of a generalization. They might rather bring to light some new factor that will drive our thinking to a further stage.

Alternatively, the kind of law which we are considering may stand as a formula, providing us with what might be called a norm; and it may not matter if in every actual historical case there is a different kind of departure from this accepted basis, this assumed norm. An important stage in what was to be the genesis of modern science was provided when Galileo broke away from the world of common-sense observations in his attempt to examine such things as the path of a projectile. The path which he discovered was one which could hardly be followed by any real projectile actually in motion in our highly intricate world; for he took the case of an imaginary body moving in purely geometrical space, without the complications of wind or air resistance. He saw that, if he could arrive at the norm, these accidental things could be caught into his system later and given their due allowance. I am not sure that much of the excellence of a good politician does not lie in the insight with which he appropriates these "norms," so that at the moment of action he has only to do the mathematical adjustment which the special circumstances of the case require.

It is not clear that the natural scientist, who today handles matters of texture with at least as much subtlety as the historian, would ever allow himself to be defeated by a further argument—sometimes regarded as the decisive one—against a science of politics. This is the argument that if men were to discover a particular law or process, their knowledge would alter their action for the future, bringing a new factor into the situation, and thereby invalidating the law itself. Perhaps the crudest example that I might quote—and I shall formulate it with the maximum crudeness—is the thesis that revolutions are subject to a process that makes them tend ever further to the left, driving them to greater and greater extremes. Without claiming validity for this thesis at the moment, we might take it as the equivalent of Galileo's attempt to discover the norm for the path of a projectile. There are some revolutions—the case of 1688 in England, and the case of 1830 in France, for example—which might lead one to have doubts about the general formula. Yet the exceptions, when they are examined, only reinforce the basic argument; for in these cases, if a check was put upon the tendency of a revolution to move out of the control of its originators, the check came from men who achieved their objective precisely because they were so aware of that fundamental tendency. We can be rigid and literalistic, saying "How can a thing be a 'law' when the mere knowledge of its existence as a 'law' makes possible its actual nullification?" And this is where the natural scientists, who can operate as though light were either a wave or a particle, and who can hold to Newton even while they allow him to have been superseded by Einstein, would not allow themselves to be nonplused. For the whole example (assuming that it is a valid one) demonstrates more clearly than before the importance of having a knowledge of this law or tendency that has been noted in revolutions. A methodical study of politics certainly would be useless if it did not enable us to take appropriate counteraction, and so to bring a further region under something like intellectual control. If we are able to prevent a revolution from rushing in a landslide ever to the left, we are still not escaping the realm of law, any more than the engineer who overrides gravity in a machine that is heavier than air. At this stage our thought may be driven to a higher altitude, our original generalization subsumed under something wider still.

It is rightly argued that an act of statesmanship must often be a work of improvization; and certainly this is the most impressive feature in the story, for every new conjuncture faces government with new and complicated combinations of circumstance. The art of taking a decision, and the moral strength required for a great resolution, are momentous features in the story, though even they may be amenable to a certain degree of analysis, and will not lose their importance by being analyzed. The methodical study of international affairs is concerned rather with the background out of which the great acts of decision emerge. One is not always sure that the judgments of political leaders arise out of a profound knowledge of the international world; and indeed there seem to be occasions when statesmen take their resolve on the experience of a single example, or, perhaps more often, in blind reaction against some single recent mistake. Even the intuition of a statesman must not be reduced to *mystique;* for it cannot exist in him full grown from the time of his birth, and it depends on his ability, not merely to live through significant events and survive them, but also to apprehend them both methodically and imaginatively. Galileo seemed to have intuitions about movement and about structures, but that had something to do with his constant experimentation in such matters. He watched the ways of projectiles, the operation of levers, and the behavior of balls on inclined planes until he seemed to know them from the inside, in the way that some men seem to know their dogs. It was said of Sir Walter Scott that he could think like a Covenanter—could reproduce the words and tones of a Covenanter in invented situations—but this again can be taken out of the realm of *mystique,* for it arose from much knowledge and experience, both of which had to be imaginatively and systematically appropriated. Even the wonderful relationship between a great pianist and his piano is a thing that must be, up to a certain point at least, amenable to analysis. The historian follows the kind of operations that we have been considering, for he delineates both men and movements, trying to disentangle the operation of conditioning circumstances, and to combine long-term views with microscopic analysis. His description of a single revolution is likely to be enriched if he brings to his study of it a knowledge of many revolutions. Certain great statesmen like Richelieu and Napoleon have revealed that they learned many things from the collation of historical data; though an inexperienced academic mind, divorced from the understanding of politics, might well go fatally wrong in such an attempt.

International affairs, then, are not merely a region for a politician's improvization. They are also a region for methodical and quasi-scientific analysis. Great mistakes are possible if governments merely live from hand to mouth; and the capacity to evaluate long-term movements may be an essential factor in the formation of a foreign policy. Human beings have their realm of freedom, which—it might be asserted—is greater than they often realize. But until they know the necessity that conditions them, they cannot know the full range of their freedom either. Whatever may be the role of science in the study of economics and sociology, this might be expected to find some parallel in the realm of political action and foreign policy. And the very fact that we analyze both our position and our condition more methodically may mean that we are able to steal a further march on events, and to subdue a wider area to our intellect and will. It may mean, therefore, a further inroad upon what otherwise is the dominion of chance.

3
History
and the Possibility of
a *Détente*

WE TODAY SEE EAST AND WEST REARED UP against one another as two mutually hostile, mutually inconsistent, systems—capitalism versus Communism, democracy versus dictatorship, Western ideals versus aggressive materialism. Many people are unable to believe that a relief from tension is within the range of the possible; they find it difficult even to imagine how such a *détente* could ever begin. Yet there have been similar conflicts between mutually exclusive systems in the past, and, after deadlock that seemed absolute and inescapable, our predecessors have in fact managed to achieve a *détente*. The thing which appears to be logically impossible, and contrary to the nature of things, may continue to produce itself out of the paradoxes of the time process. This is no guarantee that a parallel relaxation will occur between West and East, or that if it occurs it will come before we have learned the necessary lessons in the most costly way possible. But history suggests that we should be wrong to rule out the possibility in advance—wrong to refuse to co-operate in this matter with Providence or the time process.

If there is need for a methodical analysis of power or aggression or the international order, there may be some point also in examining the general problem of *détente*. Examples occur in many fields of history; and where they do not enable us to establish definite conclusions, they may suggest changes in current ideas or assumptions. Toward the close of the nineteenth century, the tension between France and Great Britain provided perhaps the most imminent threat to European peace. Within a few years, however, Great Britain was concluding with France the agreement which formed the basis of the Entente Cordiale. We cannot pretend that those topics of litigation which had produced such intensity of crisis had been spirited

61

away by a magic wand. Yet problems which had seemed amenable to no solution save that of war proved to be manageable when the powers concerned had assumed a different posture—when they had become genuinely anxious to reach an agreement. As between these two powers, therefore, a remarkable *détente* had occurred, though, in this particular case, there may have been no decrease in the pressure in Europe as a whole. The bulge in the indiarubber ball had merely been shifted to another place; and the thing which had brought the former rivals together was the greater fear that they had come to have for Germany. As China becomes more autonomous in her policies, and particularly as she becomes more formidable in herself, it is possible that Russia's relations with the West will be changed somewhat, the interplay between these two parties becoming more complicated. International tension is at its most constant when only two or three great powers—perpetually crouching like a tiger ready for the spring—hold the effective balance, each jealously watching the moves of the others. Every addition to their number, provided it represents an independent center of action, serves to complicate the relationships and so relieves the pressure on the rest.

The problems of high pressure and *détente* may occur not merely in international relations but in the internal life of a single society. A revolutionary regime, if it is radical at all, is a very precarious thing unless drastic measures are taken to maintain it. It may condemn a whole people to a long period of tyranny and tension, which are likely to be more severe and oppressive in proportion to the size of the country affected and the organization required. We have perhaps given insufficient thought to the difficulty of securing a relaxation under a revolutionary system, when the struggle for power lacks the usual mitigations, and government itself lacks the benefit of habitual and unquestioned allegiance. The processes involved are some-

what subtle, and it would appear that the men who brought
about the fall of Robespierre in 1795 were by no means in-
tending to put an end to the French Revolutionary "Terror."
Robespierre's name had come to be so popularly associated
with the Terror that, after his execution, a *détente* which was
unplanned and unintended was brought about because it was
assumed that this was the natural corollary. Instead of asking
why Khrushchev waited so long after the death of Stalin before he announced a relaxation, we ought perhaps to remember the difficulties and the risk which would be bound to attend
such an announcement. Since that time it would appear that
the struggle for power in Russia has still been more cruel and
hazardous than in the government of a regular democracy. It
is possible that Stalin allowed the high pressure to continue
longer than the situation called for. There is also a possibility,
however, that even a Khrushchev cannot produce a *détente*
merely by wanting to do so.

In order to gain an impression of the paradoxical character
of the historical processes involved, we may find it useful to
examine a chapter of history which presents the classical example of extreme tension followed by ultimate *détente*. Europe,
during the last few centuries, has had considerable experience
of creeds, ideologies and regimes whose claims were absolute.
It has already seen bitter conflicts between systems which purported to be universal, and which were mutually exclusive. The
Wars of Religion for a number of generations after Luther's
break with Rome provide perhaps the closest analogy to the
conflicts of the twentieth century.

Perhaps it is only by an effort of the historical imagination
that we today can gain any idea of the dreadfulness of the
deadlock which the religious issue—the conflict between Protestant and Catholic—produced in the sixteenth and seventeenth
centuries. To us the tremendous preoccupation with religion

may seem as artificial, and the resulting conflicts as unreal, as the quarrels of modern literary cliques about the nature of poetry. It is difficult for the twentieth century to form any vivid conception of a time when, for individuals, societies and governments, the right propitiation of the deity seemed the most momentous thing in the world. In the period with which we are concerned, the idea of eternal punishment was not a mere speculative affair. Many thought of hell as an established fact, and pictured it as a vivid, concrete reality. Those students of history who take it for granted that vested interests provide the chief motor behind human actions can hardly deny that the wrath of God, as it was believed to operate both in this world and in the next, could touch a man in his selfish concerns. Even for the egotistical, religion provided a range of human motives that were calculated to be at least as powerful as the purely economic ones.

In the period of their terrible conflict, both the Catholic and the Protestant held that the establishment of the right religion was momenous for the mundane welfare of society and also for the ultimate destiny of the individual. They were agreed on a further matter which the twentieth century does not easily apprehend. If it was important to have the right religion, it was nothing less than self-evident that only one religion could be right. If Catholicism was true, then Protestantism was a monstrous blasphemy, reared up by human presumption. If Protestantism was true, then the Pope was Antichrist, and wicked men had corrupted Christianity to serve their mundane purposes. Above all, it was unthinkable that two forms of the Christian religion could coexist within a given country. In those days the whole of society was a church as well as a state, and England was corporately Christian, with a government that was partly ecclesiastical in character—a government that was supposed to be at the service of the true faith. Protestantism and Catholicism were mutually exclusive, therefore; and in nothing were they more agreed than in the view that their coexistence was unthinkable. For a hundred and fifty years Europe was ravaged by civil wars and international conflicts which owed their cruelty and intensity to religious fanaticism.

The whole struggle is strange to us because it could not have taken place except on the basis of an assumption which we to-day find it almost impossible to understand. In that age it was difficult even to conceive the possibility of a world in which every individual was left free to choose his form of religion. The parties concerned would have felt culpable before Heaven if they had sacrificed their ideal of the New Jerusalem, their notion of a state that should be absolutely solid and unanimous in the faith. Even when there was a call for freedom of conscience, this was not understood as we understand it; for the Huguenots in France, while claiming the freedom to practice the right religion, would not concede that by the same argument they ought to tolerate Roman Catholicism when they themselves were in the ascendancy. The right to practice wrong religion and rear up a blasphemy could never stand before their eyes as a case of conscience at all.

The solution to the problem of coexistence in the age of the great religious conflict was ultimately to be found in the principle of toleration; but only after generations of suffering—and much against their will—did the religious parties accept a principle that had been initially so uncongenial to them. Once a regime of religious liberty had been established, the world breathed more freely, and it then came to be felt that a happier and more promising era had been opened for humanity. Men imagined that it was a thing which they and their predecessors had always been looking for, though in fact they had been straining to reach entirely different goals, and it needed a complicated historical process to produce the result finally attained.

In the first place, when states could not go on fighting one another any longer, they were forced to be content with an intermediate arrangement. Since neither religious party succeeded in exterminating the other, the only resort was the principle of *Cujus regio ejus religio*. Nobody had the power to coerce all princes and bring them into conformity with one another; but princes might coerce their own subjects, so that the rulers were left to decide the religion of their citizens. A prince might still find that there was a religious cleavage in his country, but even when the minority party was too formidable for mere repression, he might try to impose a policy of Comprehension on everybody, producing a compromise between Catholicism and Protestantism or a combination of elements from both. This at least seemed more acceptable than the idea of allowing a great number of the citizens of the state to form a dissident body, alien to the official religion of the country.

Toleration, when it began to appear, would come by devious routes and would be accepted for anomalous reasons. If it seemed proper that a Catholic prince-bishop should resign his see when he became a Protestant, it could be claimed on behalf of the Protestants that at least this man's subjects should not be tied to Catholicism but should be allowed to change their religion if they liked. In France, certain cities and the lands of certain great lords were allowed to practice the Protestant faith; but this meant transposing into the interior of a single country something like the principle of *Cujus regio ejus religio*. In Poland, toward the end of the sixteenth century, some of the leading Catholics showed considerable wisdom and foresight. They argued that if the government were to decree freedom not merely for a single Protestant faith but for all forms of religion, the conflict between the multitude of sects would ruin

the cause of the Reformation and leave Catholicism trium-
phant. By this time some of the Lutherans had come to hate
Calvinism more than they hated the Catholic Church; but
gradually the cause of freedom was advanced as Protestants
learned at least to tolerate one another, if only for the purpose
of combining against Catholicism as the common enemy. In
some countries a system of virtual toleration might be produced because the ruler was secular-minded, or was too weak
to enforce the ideal of religious conformity. Alternatively, he
might see the advantage of playing off one formidable religious party against another, or he might desire to avoid the
economic loss which his state would suffer if religious dissidents
emigrated. All this might take place, and, still, pious men might
be unhappy, feeling that it was wrong to permit such rents in
the seamless cloak of Christ. Only in gradual stages did religious people come to regard toleration as anything but an unfortunate *pis aller*. Some men even said that though religious
uniformity was the ideal and persecution the proper thing, it
was necessary to compromise with principle, rather than allow
a warfare that would end in the destruction of society.

Religious freedom was really made possible by wider developments in the life and thought of Europe—developments
which embraced all the conflicting parties and even altered the
whole platform on which the struggle was being waged. The
competition between religious authorities had itself tended to
undermine the very conception of authority, and exalted the
individual who was so often now in a position to choose between alternative systems. The rise of modern science did much
to discredit the particular authority which both classical antiquity and the medieval world had so long enjoyed. Partly as
a result of these developments, and partly in reaction against
excessive fanaticism and religious conflicts, a great process of
secularization occurred, and religion lost its presidency over

society and thought, the intellectual leadership passing to new classes of men who had little reverence for tradition or established systems. Many who lapsed from Christianity altogether now joined in the cry for freedom of conscience, and in general the coming of religious indifference became a factor in the development of a more tolerant world. By this time, indeed, many pious men had come to realize that there were valid reasons for differences in religious opinion, so that toleration had begun to appear also as a religious ideal, as a right of conscience, a thing commanded by the law of charity.

One of the primary conditions of any *détente*—whether in the seventeenth century or in the twentieth—is the recovery of the realization that the members of whatever may be the hostile party are human beings too, not fundamentally unlike ourselves. It is pertinent to note that if Christians had gone back to the early days of the Church and the fountain of their faith —if they had gone back to their first principles and used these as their touchstone, instead of adhering to systems that had been established in the intervening centuries—they could have achieved the same result from the first. There was no historical determinism which made it impossible to hold the ideal of religious liberty from the time of Luther's great revolt—impossible to escape a hundred and fifty years of bloodshed and atrocity that did great damage to the cause of religion itself. Men had merely allowed their Christianity to be too closely entangled with the systems and the vested interests of the world. Some, indeed, like Erasmus, had set out to stress the importance of charity and tolerance from the very first, but their policies had seemed too idealistic, too unreal. Such voices had been virtually submerged in the storm and thunder of bitter religious conflict. It is astonishing to what a degree history in the long run vindicates charity and generosity even in politics. And it may be true again today that, if we do not listen to the voice of tolerance, a long era of bloodshed may bring us only to the same result, though by so much more costly a path.

In the case of the ancient conflict of religion, as perhaps also in the case of our twentieth-century conflicts, the mere passage of generations is almost bound to have a part in the story. In the long run, history moves into a world of different ends and preoccupations, so that human beings, intent on new purposes, fail to appreciate, and fail even to understand, the objects that their predecessors fought so hard to secure. In our own time there have been people willing to fight to the utmost limit for the principle of self-determination; but the principle is liable to be inconvenient at the present day, and some of these very people now speak disparagingly of the thing they once worshiped. When posterity saw the era of religious conflict in retrospect, it regarded toleration as a creative achievement, so that it required a special effort of historical imagination to understand why pious and good men could ever have wanted anything else. The establishment of freedom of conscience came to seem like a transition to a higher order of existence. It was felt that, now, mankind had surmounted a formidable hurdle which once had blocked the progress of civilization itself.

If toleration was the solution to the problem of coexistence in the seventeenth century, after the great religious conflicts, it may require some original thinking to discover the parallel solution for the problem of coexistence in the twentieth century. If we do discover such a solution we may expect that, as in the case of toleration, it will imply an actual enlargement of human liberty somewhere. It is almost bound to mean that we allow people or peoples the right to be free in respect of certain things in which, at the present day, neither party wants to permit them the choice. We, too, may find ourselves accepting unwillingly, as a *pis aller*, something which our successors will regard as a blessing in itself.

It is better to think of *détente* after studying a single example, than simply to reason about it a priori without the knowledge of any example at all. Even on the small amount of material now before us we can come to some tentative conclusions; and, first of all, it might be suggested that the question of *détente* can hardly arise until aggression has first been checked. Short of such a check, the world simply surrenders to Protestant powers in the sixteenth century, and to Communism in the twentieth. Once the opposing parties are held in balance there may be an unsettled period during which their equality in power even acts as a further incentive to war. One of the parties—like the Protestants in post-Reformation Germany—may feel that if it makes a particularly strong effort it can turn the balance, and use the acquired momentum to rush to swift, irreversible victory. When the position begins to stabilize itself, however, peoples and governments become accustomed to settled existence—the fact that they now enjoy a little of it only makes them long for more. It is not necessarily the fear of actual defeat which checks the aggressor in any period of history; for sometimes a state will have shown a readiness to attack so long as an invasion was a mere walkover—it may have been tempted by the existence of a power vacuum. This does not necessarily mean that it ever had the intention of facing the risk or the strain of a general war.

But, even when an uneasy balance has been achieved, there can be no further progress so long as the energies of the states concerned are entirely taken up with the problem of a possible war. If government can do nothing more than fend off present dangers—if it is entirely occupied with the task of keeping head above water—the deadlock is absolute and the strain unremitting. A government may, however, continue mechanically to behave in this way—doing all its thinking with only war in mind—after the situation has begun to call for something more.

If so, it suffers from a double danger, because on the one hand it will overstrain its subjects after the reason for this has ceased to be plausible; and in such a case its system will be in danger of cataclysmic reversal at home. On the other hand, it may fail to catch up when its potential enemy shows flexibility and imagination, and embarks on a different tactic altogether.

Marxism, at this second stage in the story, has an advantage because it is a missionary creed. We must remember that it can operate inside other countries without resorting to actual violence, and it can even have its own agents amongst the natives of the countries concerned. Calvinism operated in this way in the sixteenth century, providing, from its nest in Geneva, the pattern for some of the most remarkable revolutionary procedures of our time. Democracy worked in a somewhat similar manner in the nineteenth century, with its international nests of revolution, its professional agents, and its resort to both intrigue and insurrection. Democrats have almost always regarded this with approval, and, so far as I know, few historians have agreed with Metternich, whose doctrine on the problem of international revolution was astonishingly similar to that of the Western powers today. To make the balance equal, it is required that democracy also should be a missionary cause, concerned to have the initiative and to produce changes in the world, and not merely to defend existing positions.

One further thing is clear. There came a time when Protestants and Catholics each had to recognize that the other could not be destroyed. We today, in the same manner, can recognize that Communism—though it may develop in ways that we have not foreseen—is not a thing that can be rooted out of the world. Even the defeat of Russia, and even the most peremptory orders from Moscow, could not put an end to its activity now. Sooner or later, therefore, we shall be compelled to hold to our democratic principles in one respect, and adopt the thesis *Cujus regio ejus religio,* the thesis, namely, that every nation has the right to choose its own regime. This being the case, it is best that we should recognize the situation, and not wait until we are forced to accept a principle so consistent with the fundamental ideals of democracy itself. It is wise, therefore, to make it clear that it is the democracies which insist upon a country's right to choose whether it will be Communist or anti-Communist. This attitude on our part is likely to be the surest way of securing that the uncommitted nations do not make Communism their choice. We are stronger if we genuinely favor the autonomy of all peoples than if we allow the Russians to be promoting the principle of autonomy in opposition to us. Our position is unfortunate if we commit ourselves to a regime in Iraq, and then the people of that country welcome too readily its overthrow.

In life and in history there are factors familiar to all of us which suggest that a relaxation of tension is a matter for reasonable hope. If there are powerful engines producing high pressure on one side, we must not forget that on the other side there are ordinary processes of society continually working to produce a *détente.* We must beware of the optical illusions of political history, and remember that most people, even in democracies, give only a very small part of their lives and thought to public affairs. In any case, it is not all people who can fasten their minds on one objective, keeping the elastic at stretch all the time. It is not all people who, even for a political purpose, will consent to go on sacrificing the welfare of their family, the interests of their business, their standard of living, their conception of the "good life." They have their devotion to the arts, the need for amusement, their falling in love—and all this is a great safety valve, since democracies are precarious when too many of their members are political fanatics. Even in Russia it would seem that, as peace continues, the administration has to take account of the desire of human beings for the ordinary amenities of life. Governments themselves, when they see that victory is receding—see that they cannot, without cost to themselves, snatch further profit from an especially favorable combination of circumstances—come to set a higher value on security and release from tension. They discover that everything is being kept at strain, and that they are trying the devotion of their subjects too much. Neither formidable dictators nor democratic ministries feel themselves so firmly and permanently in the saddle that they can go on ignoring such matters for an indefinite period. Governments themselves change their objectives, have short memories sometimes, and discover new bogies to fear. At one moment we try to think of a way in which to cripple Germany for ever. But within a few years we are terrified lest she should refuse to rearm. The processes of history tend to turn even revolutionary regimes into conservative ones, which seek to acquire the security of normal times, and fear the loss of whatever good they have achieved. A people may have been whipped into a state of frenzy by the danger of war or the pressures of a revolution; but every year in which they taste security makes them love security more— makes them glad to surrender to the preoccupations of ordinary life. Sometimes, for the sake of mere peace and order, nations in the past—and even incipient democracies, jaded with tumult—have surrendered to some kind of dictatorship.

The truth is that men—whether as individuals or in groups and societies—differ very greatly from one another in their predominant end or their chief preoccupation. For one it may be religion, for another socialism, for another music, for another business, for another the welfare of his family. Each may feel it not merely his right but also his duty to go to the utmost limits of aggressiveness in the promotion of his primary object. But time and human management may bring them into a curious and providential unanimity in regard to the object that comes next. Once they feel that their aggressiveness is really being held in check, both men and nations quickly find themselves on the path to the decision that peace is best. They want at least to be guarded against other aggressors; and they discover that after all it pays them to have a reasonable order of things. If the Protestant cannot have the domination of the Continent, it becomes a primary interest to him that none of his rivals shall do so either. In fact, when the Protestant or the liberal or the Communist ceases his career of exultant conquest, he prefers that the whole issue should be left to the play of reason, the crossfire of propaganda, the arbitrament of public opinion. Those who have faith in their own cause will tell themselves that they are bound to win if only they can have peace and fair play—fair opportunity to use their powers of persuasion. In proportion to their belief in their cause, they feel that in the last resort the historical process will be on their side. Though men, nations and causes are so aggressive, in the long run everybody at least wants to see everybody else subjected to the rules of a civilized world.

It was once realized, in a way in which I believe it is not realized today, that these facts throw light on the real mission of a foreign office—the function of diplomacy being prescribed by the nature of things. In so far as a state can be more than merely self-regarding, or can even be farsighted in its own interests, there is a higher creative role for foreign policy, and that is the establishment of a *modus vivendi* between opposing creeds and systems. The role is a creative one because the problem appears at first sight to be insoluble—it requires the discovery of a *modus vivendi* between systems which at the beginning of the argument are mutually exclusive, incapable of coexistence. Something may have to be achieved which is as new as the principle of "toleration" once was—something perhaps as initially repellent to most of the world because it will require a change in our basic assumptions. Let us not deceive ourselves with the notion that everything can be decided by international organs in which the Communists might know in advance that they would always be outvoted by non-Communists. The old German constitution after the age of the Reformation faced that dilemma, and took account of the fact that Protestants could not just allow themselves to be outvoted by Catholics. Christians themselves have refused to recognize this majority principle where vital vested interests were concerned. Complications would arise if on all questions relating to the Western Hemisphere the United States were asked to subject their will to that of the majority of South American republics. Nor would a highly civilized and highly responsible state accept bona fide a system under which it would be outvoted by undeveloped and irresponsible states.

Once the *modus vivendi* has been established, the higher objects of life—the issue between Protestantism and Catholicism or between Democracy and Communism—can be left to the play of reason. So much at least can be stolen out of the realm of force—no longer left at the mercy of violence and hazard, no longer consigned to the chances of war. In fact, the higher the cause—and even if the cause is that of Christianity itself—the more important it becomes to extract it from amongst the purposes of diplomacy or the objectives of belligerent powers. Cardinal Richelieu, when he governed seventeenth-century France, was both significant and successful because he conducted diplomacy and war for limited purposes, disentangling the religious from the more mundane elements in foreign policy. He could make war on the Hapsburg dynasty because it was a menace to France, but, though that dynasty was Catholic, he tried to secure that his action should not harm the cause of Catholicism. As the world emerged from the age of religious

wars it came to be recognized that there must be a more refined type of international order, not restricted like the medieval one to a single form of Christianity, but providing an arena
for the conflict of creeds and putting limits to the kind of struggle that might take place between them. The younger Pitt
fought revolutionary France because its aggressions threatened
Britain. He resisted Burke's demand for a war of religion
against revolution and democracy as such.

Neither Catholicism nor Protestantism surrendered anything
that was essential to its faith when they entered the new order
of things that succeeded the wars of religion. They have retained all that they regarded as necessary for a man's salvation,
and neither has given up even the claim to be right, the claim
to the exclusive possession of the truth. They have abandoned
only extraneous principles which had given them the power to
coerce all dissidents and to make war on a religious pretext. In
the end the greatest paradox of all takes place: the Protestants
have been influenced in more recent times by Catholic thought;
a Catholic historian has traced his own ideal of liberty to the
seventeenth-century Protestant sects; the two religious parties
sharpened their scholarship on one another in the period of
mutual criticism and bitter controversy; and nowadays they
stand in many respects as allies against the paganism of the
world. Instead of each regarding the other as a monolithic system, a continuous slab of evil, it is better that each should regard the other as a complex of ideas, each specifying in detail
where the other has gone wrong. When we take this view we
make the discovery that a cause which embodies much good,
and which seeks the good, may be led into diabolical cruelty by
some single idea which it has taken into its system. This was
true of both Catholicism and Protestantism in the age of the
wars of religion, and, curiously enough, though each reproached
the other for its persecutions and atrocities, the chief evils re-

sulted from the very ideas that the two held in common. Ideas which had once been understandable, and which had their attractive side, led both religious parties to considerable cruelties and persecutions. I do not know that the evils of the present day are due to a heresy which characterises both the democratic and the communistic systems; but I am sure that one of the things we now most resent in Communism—its resort to wild agitation, intrigue and insurrectionary methods—is a heresy which it shares with the earlier, revolutionary stage of the democratic ideal, and which it borrowed directly from the traditions of revolutionary democracy. The process of *détente,* which can be hastened or delayed by the conduct of statesmen on both sides, is completely held up so long as each rival party regards the other as a monolithic slab of unredeemed evil. It is better that each should regard the other as representing a mixture of ideas, and each steal the best from the other.

Precisely because the need of the world is so great, a diplomacy which merely envisages the conflict with Communism comes short of that high function which it has attained in our civilization. We have to defend ourselves; but we have to meet also what is perhaps the extreme problem of politics and international affairs: namely, the question how the world is to be steered out of an era of war, or a country out of a revolutionary situation. This problem of *détente* is not even confined to the realm of foreign policy, for one of the grave objections to the revolutionary form of procedure is the transition to dictatorship and the difficulty of restoring conditions of what we should call normality.

Whether we are practicing diplomacy, therefore, or conducting a war, or negotiating a peace treaty, or dealing with public opinion, we ought to have one ultimate objective, to which all our more immediate aims should have reference. Our purpose should be the development and maintenance of an international order which properly embraces all the competing nations, systems, creeds and ideologies. This is more particularly incumbent on those who hold the democratic ideal and concede to the various peoples of the world the right of self-determination. We have to work for this even if the other party is not working for it; and we cannot leave anybody out of the system, cannot send any nation or creed or regime or ideology to Coventry. If we exclude any of these from the club we are at least giving them the license to behave as they like; and, if we say we will have no truck with them, we exempt them from the obligation to play the game according to the rules.

4
Human Nature and the Dominion of Fear

FEAR IS A THING WHICH IS EXTRAORDINARILY vivid while we are in its grip; but once it is over, it leaves little trace of itself in our consciousness. It is one of the experiences that we can never properly remember—one, also, which since we may be ashamed of it we may have reason for not wishing to remember. We are in the position of those unsympathetic parents who, though they can recall the concrete things that happened in their lives, have forgotten what it really felt like to be in love. It is curious that moods and sensations which mastered us in the past, and which may almost consume a man, are so difficult to recover or to reimagine afterward.

Because it is so hard for us to recapture the feeling in our imagination, we can be thoroughly nonparticipating when there is question of a fear that is not our own. If another person is the victim of it, we may fail—or it may never occur to us to try—to apprehend either the thing in itself or the range of its possible consequences. It would seem that we are not always easily convinced of the existence of fear in other people, especially when the other people are political rivals or potential enemies. At any rate historians are not easily convinced when they deal at a later time with former enemies of their country. Above all, if the thing which the other party dreaded is a danger that never materialized, it becomes easy to be skeptical about the genuineness of the fear itself. When the historian cannot escape recording the terror that Napoleon inspired, or the German dread of Russia at one time and another, or the apprehension of a people in the face of imminent attack, he may produce a factual statement that gives little impression of the force and the effect of the emotion actually experienced. Sometimes he is jolted into a realization of his deficiency as he finds himself confronted by an event and sees that the rest of his picture provides only an inadequate context for it. It turns out that there was some standing factor in the story—a terrible feeling of thunder in the atmosphere—which he had imperfectly apprehended or merely failed to keep in mind. We read of Londoners who, during the Gordon Riots, pandered to the forces of anarchy; they felt it safer to don the blue cockade of the rioters than to rely on government protection. We learn that when Robespierre spoke before the revolutionary Convention on the day preceding his fall, his vague charges and threats against unspecified traitors left every man in apprehension—wondering whether his own life was safe; and for this reason he lost his majority. When we meet such things as these we are sometimes forced to the sudden realization of the fact that the story has been going on for some time in an atmosphere of fear which we have been failing to take sufficiently into account. Through such pinholes there leaks evidence of a terror which clearly underlies a wider area of the narrative than the single episode that drew our attention to it.

The student of history needs to consider this question, therefore. Some aspects of the past—and these perhaps the ones most related to men's minds and moods—are particularly difficult to recapture. The atrocities of our own day, for example, are naturally more vivid to us than those of a century ago. The world tends to judge a present-day revolution merely by its atrocities and an ancient one much more by its ideals and purposes. This is partly because the sufferings and terrors of a former generation are more easily overlooked. We need to possess something of the art of the dramatist in order to enter into the sensations of other people—to recover, for example, the "feel" of some terror that once possessed a nation or a ministry. And it must not be said that we ought to leave our imagination out of our history, for the minds of men, and even the mood of society, may have their part in accounting for human conduct.

Even when the student of the past is really bent on analysis, he must recapture the fear, and the attendant high pressure, which so greatly affect the actions of men and the policy of governments. Yet the historical imagination is never so defective as when it has to deal with the apprehension and insecurity of frightened people. It is a point to remember, therefore, that the historian, surveying the past (like the statesman surveying rival powers in his own contemporary world), is apt to do less than justice to the part played by fear in politics, at any rate so far as concerns governments other than his own.

We do not always realize—and sometimes we do not like to recognize—how often a mistaken policy, an obliquity in conduct, a braggart manner, or even an act of cruelty, may be traceable to fear. What is true of individual people is likely to be still more true of great agglomerations of humanity, where further irrational factors always come into play. With nations, even more than with individuals, in fact, the symptoms of fear may be unlike fear—they may even be the result of an attempt to convince us of the reverse. Apart from all this, fear may exist as a more constant and less sensational factor in life, perpetually constricting very reasonable people in their conduct in the world. It may curb their natural desire to react against injustice, or (if only by the production of wishful thinking) prevent them from recognizing the crimes of their own government. It can lead to small compliances and complicities, the production of "yes men," the hardening of inherited orthodoxies and accepted ideas. It may cause a man to halt in the course of his own speculations, and shrink from the dreadful audacity of pushing his thought to its logical conclusion. Even in the field of scholarship, writers may be too frightened of one another; historians may be too anxious to play safe. There can also be a generalized fear that is no longer conscious of being fear, and hangs about in the form of oppressive dullness or heavy cloud, as though the snail had retreated into its shell and forgotten the reason, but had not the spirit to put out its feelers any more.

Sir Edward Grey said that it was unwise for a diplomat to be oversuspicious. It is possible that he himself was most unfortunate in the region where he failed to follow his own teaching. During the French Wars of Religion, the fear, the whisperings and the rumors of atrocities—the deadlock of suspicion and countersuspicion—produced the atmosphere of melodrama; and this psychological fever seems to have had the effect of multiplying the atrocities. There was a time when ministers in France were formidable potentates, who knew that on their fall they would be pursued for their enormities or persecuted for their mistakes. So long as this situation endured, the ministers, therefore, would try to entrench themselves in dynastic systems; they would resort to desperate measures in order to keep their power. The result was that when Mazarin engaged in intrigue, Louis XIV rather charitably excused him on the ground that this was natural for a man in his position. Later, when Louis had drawn the claws of ministers and put them on something more like their modern footing, he said that they actually preferred the new conditions of things, because they could work in greater confidence and security. Political strife must have been mitigated even in England when ministers could retire from office without having to fear that they would be impeached by those who supplanted them. Here, too, the transition from the politics of melodrama, the politics of the *coup d'état,* was achieved in proportion as fear was reduced. The extreme case, however, is the situation that Hobbes seems to have had in mind—a situation in which men are not absolutely brutish, and do not want to be brutish, but are made brutish by their fear and suspicion of one another. Each may be wanting peace above all things, but no single one of them can be certain about the intentions of the rest. They are like two men in a room, both anxious to throw their pistols away, but in a state of deadlock because each must be sure that he does not disarm himself before the other.

In other words, fear and suspicion are not merely factors in the story, standing on a level with a lot of other factors. They give a certain quality to human life in general, condition the nature of politics, and imprint their character on diplomacy and foreign policy. Over and over again during the course of the French Revolution fear and suspicion—fear of the foreign invader, but also suspicion of aristocratic plots—underlie the development of the story and decide the turn of events.

It is the realm of international affairs, however, which comes closest to the last situation that has been mentioned, the situation of Hobbesian fear. Since the war of 1914 our predicament in this respect has become worse, not better, because, till that time, a considerable region of Europe had long enjoyed the benefit of stability and traditional acceptance. Here frontiers had been comparatively settled and a country like Norway had not needed to be greatly preoccupied with its security. Much of that region has now been thrown into the melting pot. It is doomed to suffer further dislocations if ever there is a change in the distribution of power. The demand for security, and the high consciousness that we now have of this problem of security, have increased the difficulty, and increased the operation of fear in the world. Hitler demanded security for Germany, and I am not sure that he did not show more discernment about this matter than many other people. It was impossible, however, for Germany to acquire the degree of security she thought she ought to have, without herself becoming a menace to her neighbors. This universe always was unsafe, and those who demand a watertight security are a terrible danger in any period of history. I wonder if it could not be formulated as a law that no state can ever achieve the security it desires without so tipping the balance that it becomes a menace to its neighbors. The great aggressors of modern times, France, and then Germany and then Russia, began by resisting aggressors, then demanding guarantees and more guarantees, until they had come almost imperceptibly to the converse position. Then the world (always rather late in the day) would wake up and find that these powers were now aggressors themselves. The French Revolution, like the Russian one, established client-republics around its frontiers, but then these had to be guaranteed, and constantly it transpired that the aggressor needed to go further in order to keep what he had already got. Napoleon, when he brought all this to a climax by going to Moscow, made arrogant assertions in his public pronouncements. In more private statements, however, one meets the hint that he knew himself to be making a gamble. Even Napoleon could be moved by fear—for he felt that everything would collapse if he failed to go forward and meet the Russian challenge.

There was a time when it was impossible to convince people that any power except Germany would be so wicked as to keep up armaments and force everybody else to be armed. It was considered meanness to suggest that another power—particularly Soviet Russia—could possibly behave in the same way; and because of that fallacy we have to face the emergence of Russian power in the twentieth century in conditions unusually disadvantageous for us. Yet, if Russia were to promise to abolish all armaments, even bows and arrows, I doubt whether we would make an agreement with her on those terms, much as we might imagine ourselves to be ready for it. We should say that the Russians, by virtue of their excess in population and by virtue of geographical contiguity, would be able to march into Europe, though they only had sticks and stones with which to fight. Indeed, there is no security for Western Europe unless America has the power to make Russia insecure. And this gives us one of the patterns of those terrible dilemmas which seem always to be confronting us in international affairs.

Further than this, the United States at the present day must be vividly aware of the fact that when a country enjoys power and predominance, even its own virtues do not exempt it from suspicion and undeserved mistrust. If this can happen when America is so necessary for the defense of the rest of the world against the Communist menace, what would happen if Communism collapsed, and if the United States were left as a single giant, lording it alone in the world? Stalin might have been the most virtuous of rulers in 1945, but the fear and suspicion would still have existed, because, for one thing, how easy it would have been for us to say that we could never be sure about the character of his successors. When a country achieves a position of predominance—a position which enables it to assert its will in many regions with impunity—not only does it imagine that its will is more righteous than it really is, but internal forces are likely to throw to the top the kind of man who will exploit the opportunity for aggression. We do not need to deny that one state, one government or one ruler may be more wicked than another; but this is simply an additional factor in the case, and it is better to regard it as superimposed upon an initial fundamental dilemma. We cannot penetrate to the roots of fear if we merely condemn the other party moralistically. It is necessary to attack rather the structure of that fundamental dilemma which is the prime cause of international deadlock.

One of the most terrible consequences of fear and war fever is a melodramatic kind of myth-making which has been the curse of international relations since 1914. This is the source of the blight which makes compassion wither out of the world; and its results are before our eyes. Because we thought that there could never be an aggressor so wicked as Germany under the Kaiser, we determined to fight the First World War to the point of total surrender. We thereby conjured into existence two menaces still more formidable for ourselves—the Communist on the one hand, the Nazi on the other. Some men realized, even in 1914, that all we needed to do was to hold off Germany till the Russian Bear became a more formidable threat to all of us. To judge by the writings of some leading members of the British Foreign Office at the time, the intervening period would not have had to be long. In general, however, we can say that, until 1914, the world was perhaps proceeding very tolerably, save that it was beginning to get a little fevered, because, already, it had come somewhat under the dominion of fear. Those who made dark and dismal prophecies about Germany could claim in the days of Hitler that their predictions had come true. But these people had their part in the producing of that nightmare situation in which their prophecies were almost bound to come true.

Fear, then, plays a greater part in life and in the course of history than we often realize, and sometimes we know that it is fear which is in operation when individuals and nations are bullying or bragging, or taking a crooked course. It may even be fear that is at work when a nation is desperately engaged in trying to convince us that it is not afraid. In spite of this (or perhaps rather because of it) one may feel a little anxious about the way in which the great powers of the earth appear to be relying on fear today. On the one hand, statesmen ought never to be too sure about the efficacy of fear in the last resort. On the other hand it is always dangerous to assume that fear can be used to cast out fear. The mere dread of having to suffer the consequences of the hydrogen bomb is not going to deter governments and peoples from starting warlike action, or intensifying this, once it has begun. In the critical instance—the case of the ruthless man who knows that he is beaten—the mere fear of retaliation will not in itself prevent desperate policies, including the actual use of the bomb.

The world can hardly ever have been so apprehensive as since the days when statesmen proclaimed that by victory in war they could bring about "freedom from fear." Those who can boast of their stocks of hydrogen bombs are not exempt from this fear, which numbs people and makes them think that they must take their fate passively, that their opinions and resolves can make no difference. We must not imagine that all is well if our armaments make the enemy afraid; for it is possible that, at least in the twentieth century, it is fear more than anything else which is the cause of war. Until very recently we ourselves had not lost the realization of the fact that mounting armaments, because they intensified fear and poisoned human relations, operated rather to provoke war than to prevent it. Under the high pressure which fear induces, any minor and peripheral issue can seem momentous enough to justify a great war.

Those who refuse to recognize squarely the dominion of fear and the play of necessity in the world (especially during times of war, revolution and unsettlement) are often the very ones who refuse to do justice to man's freedom when they are called upon for an act of will. It is for this reason that a world as intellectually advanced as ours stands mute and paralyzed before a great issue; and we grind our way, content to be locked in historical processes, content just to go digging our thought deeper into whatever happens to be the accustomed rut. There comes a moment when it is a healthy thing to pull every cord tight and make an affirmation of the higher human will. When we seem caught in a relentless historical process, our machines enslaving us, and our weapons turning against us, we must certainly not expect to escape save by an unusual assertion of the human spirit. The intensified competition in armaments embodies movements which have been mounting through the centuries, and providing mankind with its chief headache for a number of decades. Those who once thought it cynical to imagine that any power save Germany could be responsible for keeping the world still in arms, and now think that only Communists could be so wicked, do not realize that if Russia and China were wiped out, the world would soon be rearming again, and, as likely as not, the United States would be getting the blame for it. In other words, the problem of armaments is a bigger one than is generally realized, and we cannot begin to put the initial check upon the evil—we cannot begin to insert the first wedge—unless we make a signal call upon every human feeling we possess. We wait, perhaps, for some Abraham Lincoln who will make the mightiest kind of liberating decision.

Here is a spacious and comprehensive human issue, at what may well be one of the epic stages in the world's history. It is a matter not to be settled in routine consultations between governments and their military experts who are always bent on going further and further in whatever direction they have already been moving. At such a crisis in the world's history, even those of us who never had any superstitious belief in human rectitude will have some faith in humanity to assert—some heart-throb to communicate—so that, across all the Iron Curtains of the world deep may call unto deep. There is aggression; there is tyranny; there is revolutionary ferment; but if we wish to civilize international affairs we must do more than arrogantly hold our own against the barbarians, merely meeting them with their own weapons. Everything is going to depend in fact upon what we do over and above the work of self-defense. There can be no international system until somebody finds a way of relieving the pressure and begins the task of creating confidence.

If it is possible to put a personal opinion without claiming any authority for it, or asserting that it ought to have any weight, but regarding it as one of the varied views that are thrown up in a democracy, one might suggest that what is most terrifying of all in the present situation is not to have to keep discovering the crimes of the Communists; it is something much more inconvenient to us: namely, having to recognize the services which Communism has rendered in various parts of the globe. Those services have been accompanied by tyranny and oppression; but, again, it is terrifying to have to remember that this was once the chief objection to revolutionary democracy. It is not even clear that Communism, though it can be so oppressive today, does not possess colossal potentialities for future liberty—a liberty that we must not expect to be achieved before an international *détente* has made it more possible to have a relaxation at home. I think that, in this modern world, which in some ways is worse than people think but in some ways is better, all systems are going to move in the direction of liberty, if only somebody will open a window so that the world can breath a more relaxed air and we can end the dominion of fear. If, however, we are unable to achieve this, the very measures which we are taking to preserve liberty in the world are bound to lead to the loss of liberty even in the regions that most prize it. They are bound—if we go on intensifying them—to make us become in fact more and more like the thing we are opposing. Even those who customarily try to guard themselves against a facile and unrealistic idealism in politics might well wonder whether—now that the hydrogen bomb has been superadded—their antidoctrinairism is not becoming too doctrinaire. When there is a question of a weapon so destructive, the risk which accompanies one kind of action has to be balanced against the risks involved in the opposite policy, or attendant upon inaction itself. When the hazard is very great in either case, it may be useful to take account also of the end for the sake of which one chooses to accept the hazard.

The hydrogen bomb will presumably always have at least a potential existence in our civilization, since the knowledge of how to make the weapon can hardly be unlearned, except in a disaster that would follow its drastic use. If we were to resort to the most destructive kind of bomb, we could hardly claim privilege for our generation or rely on any possibility of restricting the use of the weapon to a single war. We cannot argue still again that no generation past or future could possibly have to face an enemy as wicked as our present enemy. We should have to conclude that ours is a civilization that took a wrong turn long ago, and now, by the hydrogen bomb, had to be rolled back to its primitive stages, so that, in a second Fall of Man, the world could unload itself of knowledge too dangerous for human possession. It is not necessary to take a very high perspective on these matters; it is just too crazy and unseemly when a civilization as lofty as ours (pouring the best of its inventive genius into the task) carries the pursuit of destructiveness to the point at which we are now carrying it. Let us be clear about one important fact: the destructiveness which some people are now prepared to contemplate is not to be justified for the sake of any conceivable mundane object, any purported religious claim or supramundane purpose, or any virtue that one system of organization can possess as against another. It is very questionable whether, when it comes to the point, any responsible leader of a nation will ever use the hydrogen bomb in actual warfare, however much he may have determined in advance to do so. The weapon is dangerous to the world because it is a weapon only for men like the falling Hitler—desperate men making their last retreat. The real danger will come from the war leader who will stick at nothing because he knows that he is defeated and doomed in any case. He may be reckless even of his own nation, determined to postpone his own destruction for a week, or to carry the rest of the world down with him. As in the case of Germany when Hitler was falling, war may be protracted by the will of a handful of wicked and desperate men. On these terms we are going to be more afraid of defeating our enemy than of suffering ordinary military defeat ourselves.

It is not clear that there is much point in having the equality (or even the superiority) in terroristic weapons if, as is sometimes asserted, the enemy has the ruthlessness and the organization to carry on a war with less regard for the sufferings of his people than is possible in the democracies. If Communism is a monstrous sadistic system, the gentle and the urbane will not easily outdo it in the use of terroristic device. By a reversal of all previous ideas on the subject of armaments, however, some people have imagined that the hydrogen bomb is the climax of blessing, the magical "deterrent" which will paralyze the guns and neutralize the numbers of the potential enemy. Such reasoning is precarious; and we ought to be very careful before we accept the view that ten years ago it was only the atomic bomb which deterred the Russians from a major war. A country in the position that Russia held after 1945 tends to seek to make use of its interim advantage up to any point short of a renewal of general war. It seeks to step in wherever there is a power vacuum and it probes for a power vacuum even where none exists—probes until it meets an uncomfortable degree of resistance. There seems to be no reason for believing that Russia would have meditated a full-scale war, even if she had had to meet only pre-atomic weapons, the weapons of Hitler's war. Short of such a conflict, I wonder what power ever went further in the type of aggrandizement in question than Russia at a time when the West held the atomic bomb while the East was still without it. It is even possible that we hoaxed ourselves with the atomic bomb, which was too monstrous a weapon for peripheral regions and problems, too terrible to use

in a cause that was in any way dubious, too cumbrous for dealing with a power that was ready to skirmish with any danger
short of actual war. In such a case one can even conceive the
possibility of the Russians realizing the situation in advance,
and calling our bluff while we ourselves were not yet aware
that we were merely bluffing. Whether this has already happened or not, it is just this situation—with the West deceived
and the Russians undeceived—that we ought to be careful to
avoid at the present day. We cannot contemplate—we cannot
even plausibly threaten—a nuclear war over some of the mixed
and mongrel issues which are arising (and are going to arise)
in sundry sections of the globe. If it is argued that we can, and
that the dread of this will be effective with the Russians, then,
beyond question, the Russians are in a more general sense under
the dominion of fear; for in such a case they have a right also
to fear a willful and capricious use of nuclear weapons.

Some men say that the world must perish rather than that
Justice should fail—as though we were not leaving sufficient
injustices unremedied on our own side of the Iron Curtain. The
justice of man has less mercy than the justice of God, who did
not say that because of the sin of some men the whole human
race should lose even the chance of bettering itself in future.
Even in peacetime the hydrogen bomb has made such a deep
impression as to suggest enormous evils (greater than the evils
of Communism itself) if the weapon is ever used by either
party in a war. The demoralizing effect on the user as well as
the victim might well include a hysteria beyond all measure,
the dissolution of loyalty to the state, and anarchy or revolution
of an unprecedented kind. Even the sense of the possible proxi-
mate use of the hydrogen bomb—short of an actual explosion
—will have the effect of creating a deep separation between
peoples and their governments. We may know that war is near
by two signs: firstly, when people begin to say that the hydro-

gen bomb is not so terrible after all; and secondly, when we are told that it is better to destroy civilization than to tolerate some piece of barbarism on the part of that nation which happens to be the potential enemy at the moment. In fact, we have reached the point at which our own weapons have turned against us, because their destructiveness is so out of relation with any end that war can achieve for mankind.

There is so great a risk in having the hydrogen bomb that there can hardly be greater risk if we unplug the whole system, and if our governments refuse to have anything to do with the weapon. Even if there were, the radical difference in the quality of these risks would cancel it; for with modern weapons we could easily put civilization back a thousand years, while the course of a single century can produce a colossal transition from despotic regimes to a system of liberty. I am giving a personal view; but I am not sure that the greatest gift that the West could bring to the world would not be the resolution neither to use the hydrogen bomb nor to manufacture it any further. Certainly the East would hardly believe us (at least for some time) if we said that we were not going to resort to this weapon for any conceivable end. We should have to take the line, therefore, that our determination was not dependent on anything that other people believed. Even if the East refused to join us in the assertion, we can declare that the hydrogen bomb is an unspeakable atrocity, not to be used in any war, and not even to be the basis of any form of threat. It is a thing not to be used even if the enemy has used it first, since the situation is a new one—the right of retaliation could mean no more than the right to multiply an initial catastrophe that could not be undone. While it is still open to us in time of peace, we might ask ourselves whether there is no conceivable weapon that we will brand as an atrocity, whether there is no horror that we should regard as impermissible for the winning of a war, because so

incommensurate with the limited objects that can ever be se-
cured by war. When we talk about using the hydrogen bomb
to defeat aggression, we are using dangerous language. Some
day, no doubt, a wiser world than ours will use the term "aggressor" against any people which enjoys rights, powers and
possessions in a country that is not its own, and exploits these
against the will of the population concerned. Sometimes we
seem to be using the term in respect of peoples who are merely
seeking to be freed from such oppression; in this sense I have
seen the Algerian rebels described as aggressors, using violence
for the purpose of securing a change in the *status quo*. The
Anglo-French action at Suez should open our eyes to the fact
that a so-called "invasion" (though it be by armies in full ar-
ray) can arise from something much more complicated than a
mere cruel lust for conquest. The United Nations condemned
the Anglo-French enterprise; but, even so, a hydrogen bomb
on London or Paris would have been an unspeakable form of
punishment.

It is sometimes argued that those who refuse to resort to the
hydrogen bomb may be declining to risk themselves for the
liberty of others. But nobody can calculate—and perhaps only
accidental circumstances would decide in a given case—whether
the use of the bomb or its repudiation would carry the greater
immediate risk. In any case, we cannot say that we will not
receive the bomb—we can only say that we will not be responsible for the sin and the crime of delivering it. Supposing we
do have to receive it, the one thing we can do is to choose the
end for which we will consent to be sacrificed. We can choose
the cause on behalf of which we will die if we are going to
have to die. We can do this instead of being the blind victims
of historical processes, which will end by making us more and
more like the thing that we are opposing. However hard we
have tried in the twentieth century to make allowances in ad-

vance for the unpredictable consequences of war, we have always discovered that the most terrible of these had been omitted from our calculations or only imperfectly foreseen. One of the examples of the fact is the loss of liberty in various countries in Eastern Europe and the Balkans—the very regions whose freedom was the primary issue for which we were supposed to have undertaken two world wars.

If it is wrong to tip the balance slightly in favor of humanity and faith at such a point as this, the fact is so monstrous as to imply the doom of our civilization, whatever decision we take on the present issue. If we picture a long line of future generations we can hardly help feeling that, even if wars of some sort continue (human nature remaining very much as it is now), we would want our successors not to hate one another so much as to think it justifiable to use the hydrogen bomb. The fact that we can contemplate such an atrocity is a symptom of a terrible degeneracy in human relations—a degeneracy which the predicament itself has no doubt greatly helped to produce. But if all this is not correct, and if we do not signally repudiate the hydrogen bomb, it is still true that in the last resort some strong human affirmation of a parallel kind may be the only way of stopping the tension and deflecting the course of development to which we are now enslaved. Some other kind of affirmation might serve a similar purpose; and amongst the possibilities at our disposal there is one which to many earnest people would come no doubt as a serious test. We have talked a great deal about the crimes of Communism, and those who are chiefly concerned with militaristic propaganda would like us to think of nothing else. We do not always realize what a tremendous area of our thinking is affected by the fact that we refuse to recognize also the services which Communism has rendered in various parts of the globe. At the very beginning of all our arguments and decisions, it matters very much if we consent to say that Communism is a benevolent thing gone wrong—it is not mere unredeemed and diabolical evil. For anything I know, its chief error may even be the same as that of both Catholics and Protestants in the age of the religious wars and persecutions—an error which has been responsible for terrible massacrings and atrocities in history—namely, a righteousness that is too stiff-necked and a readiness to believe that one can go to any degree in the use of force on behalf of a cause that one feels to be exclusively right. In such a case it is possible that we ourselves are making even the identical error, especially in any contemplation of the use of the hydrogen bomb. When there is a terrible *impasse,* it is sometimes useless to go on battering against the obstruction—one must play a trick on fatality by introducing a new factor into the case. We seem unable to subdue the demon of frightfulness in a head-on fight. Let us take the devil by the rear, and surprise him with a dose of those gentler virtues that will be poison to him. At least when the world is in extremities, the doctrine of love becomes the ultimate measure of our conduct.

All this represents in any case the kind of way in which to assert the human will, against the machinery of relentless process, in history. It represents also the way in which one would like to see the Christian religion working softly and in silence upon the affairs of the world at large. It illustrates the way in which religious activity may get a purchase on the wheels of a human destiny which otherwise now appears to be directionless.

5
Christianity
and Global Revolution

AT THE BEGINNING OF THE FIFTEENTH CENTURY
Christendom had ceased to expand, but Islam was advancing
into Europe and had a formidable position in the world. The
Ottoman Turks had opened their career of European conquest,
and much of Asia was falling under the dominion of the Crescent, or suffering from Mohammedan pressure. The Moors had
gained control of the commerce of the Asiatic seas, and were
becoming masters of the production of spices as well as the
trade in this merchandise, which was of crucial importance to
the West. The rulers of Cairo stood across an important route
between Europe and India; and when the Venetian traders
picked up their goods in Alexandria or in Syria, these wares
had suffered colossal increases in price, owing to the transit
through many jurisdictions, and the repeated transshipments
that had to take place. Africa itself, in so far as it was known
at that time, seemed open to Islam, save for a Christian outpost
in Abyssinia. The conflict between the Cross and the Crescent
had reached a grim and frightening stage; and it is not easy
to explain why Western Christendom came to prevail in the
next one hundred and fifty years.

This global conflict, because it underlies so much of the history of the fifteenth century, gives a new dimension to the epic
of that age, the cumulative achievements of the Age of Discovery. It would seem that the Europeans beat the Arabs at their
own game when they developed their nautical skill and under-
took those voyages which finally brought Columbus to America
and Vasco da Gama to India. One of the curious problems of
history is the question why the Portuguese, with a handful of
men and a handful of ships, managed to gain control of the
Asiatic seas and corner the trade of the Spice Islands for themselves. It was not merely through the quaintness or fantasy of

the medieval mind that the great discoveries could appear as an aspect or a by-product of the Crusades. The fight between the Cross and the Crescent drove Christians into learning more about the globe, and before they quite knew what they were doing, they had acquired a general ascendancy in the world.

When German historians at the end of the eighteenth century began to map out a system of what they called "universal history," they saw the whole period since Columbus as an era characterized by this global predominance of Western Europe. They were soon attributing it in part to the development of the system of European states and the actualization in the West of an effective idea of the state, compared with which the whole Asiatic order of things seemed amorphous and astonishingly weak. A brilliant Arabic civilization had preceded the remarkable rise of Western culture in the Middle Ages; but this, too, had declined, and the West, though it had started later, had soon proved to be the more dynamic. In the fifteenth century, at the very time of the great discoveries, the stimulus which the Renaissance gave to Western culture, and the fall of Constantinople before the Turks, made more apparent the cultural leadership which Western Europe had in many respects already attained.

Even now, the West did not achieve security for a long time, because the Turks remained a menace for nearly two centuries more. They continued to advance out of the Balkans and in 1526 they acquired much of Hungary, after which they besieged Vienna more than once. In 1683 they came westward in great force and had a plausible hope of reaching the Rhine. Not until 1683 was the tide turned, so that henceforward it was the infidel who was on the defensive in Europe. A colossal conflict between Europe and Asia had played its part in the downfall of the ancient Roman Empire in the West. After that, for nearly fifteen hundred years, this struggle between the continents was perhaps the most tragic of what might be called the standing features of world history. Before it had finished, it had turned into a backward region those eastern Mediterranean lands which had been the cradle of our civilization and had kept for thousands of years the cultural leadership over a great section of the globe. This conflict between Europe and Asia, and the resulting disaster for the intermediate region, is a further reason for the great predominance which the West acquired. Once again it was perhaps the structure of power politics in Western Europe, and the organization of the Western form of state, which put a halt to the advance of the infidel, and kept the Turks east of Vienna.

The supremacy which was acquired by Western Europe found its characteristic embodiment in colonial and imperialistic systems. It was the emigrants from the Old World—led by the thirteen colonies of North America—who set the example of the revolt against European overlordship—rebellion in the first place against "the mother country." In the British Empire there developed the doctrine that not merely the emigrants —not merely the British colonists and their descendants in Canada, for example—but also the native populations of India and Africa were being trained for future responsibility and self-government. The process of emancipation has sometimes been very slow and has undoubtedly been checked by various forms of vested interest, but the British ministers have on occasion shown a political generosity which has forestalled the most serious forms of military conflict. If there have been regions in which nothing less than agrarian revolution (for example) would have been capable of solving problems of life and death, the old imperial systems of the Western European states have never had the dynamic for this. On occasion they have even been too content to patronize ancient abusive regimes and to make alliance with a decadent order of things.

Sometimes they have felt it a virtue to allow subject peoples to continue in their customary mode of life; and in the light of our present knowledge of the world's potentialities, we might have to say that, in Asia and Africa, the Western powers, for some decades now, have been moving at too slow a pace. England herself seems to have done a good deal to train the very men who were later to rebel against her. The present ideals of the Indians or the Arabs or the Africans had been taken over from Europe to a considerable degree before Communism really entered the picture. Now, however, the emergence of political consciousness over wide areas of the globe has shaken the very basis of the older kind of paternal imperialism. It has undermined the supposed right of the more advanced peoples to withhold liberty and autonomy even for prudential reasons or educational purposes. It is the impact of the West which has awakened the backward, or the undeveloped, or the subject peoples; and now the call for an accelerated pace of progress is irresistible. The technique of a revolutionary age has provided more swift and drastic—if also more cruel—ways of galvanizing these peoples and putting an end to moribund regimes.

Some of us believe that revolution would be a disaster for the highly civilized states of Western Europe because it would destroy so many imponderable things. We can see that materialism and egotism can be organized into monstrosities which are a menace to civilization, capable of destroying values that have taken centuries to produce. We must not be too sure, however, that this type of argument is entirely applicable to great areas of the globe where newly awakened peoples are just discovering that their miseries are not irremediable. These masses may find their material need so desperate as to make mere "liberty"—the mere freedom of the ballot box—seem doctrinaire and unreal. Revolution perhaps always has its cruelties and evils, but it may not necessarily involve for all peoples the sacrifice of an achieved political liberty of the kind that Western Europe enjoys. Some peoples have never really known freedom and autonomy; they may be incapable of self-government; they may need radical change but may have to be brought to it by a new kind of paternalism— not the paternalism of an overlord who is interested in keeping things as they are. When one considers their position one is inclined to marvel that Africans, and other struggling and dependent peoples, have not succumbed to the Communist ideal more than they have done. And at the moment of the Communist success in China, who could help having what was perhaps an irrational and unavoidable feeling of terror? After seeing that country suffer a long succession of pointless miseries and fruitless upheavals, one realized that now, at last, she was going to be put on her feet and set on a course of development that was bound to make her formidable to the rest of us. So far as the area of ancient Christendom is concerned, Communism, in certain of its aspects, seems to represent a decline in civilization. From this point of view the effect of two world wars has been to bring that decline into the heart of Europe and to give a tremendous predominance and leadership to a less civilized section of the globe. It is not so clear that Communism would represent a similar decline, or an equivalent degree of it, in some of the less developed areas of the globe. Though it behaves oppressively, it may surpass the states of Western Europe in its ability to awaken, organize and develop backward countries and undeveloped peoples.

In any case, Western Europe has now lost the privileged position which it enjoyed for something like five centuries. There is a wider Western world, led by the United States, but even this has lost its monopoly in modern civilization, and its political and cultural leadership. We have been losing ground over much of the globe but we have been losing it to something which itself is essentially Western in character. Communism and Marxism in particular are European products, and if China goes Communist she still comes under the influence of a culture that is astonishingly Western. It is possible for us to lose faith in ourselves and forget the way in which the Asiatic continent has surrendered to the West, taking over our science, our technology, our political ideals, our diplomatic traditions, our governmental practices, and many of our ideas about life. This must rank as the greatest disappointment of our whole era, for some of us have dreamed from our earliest youth that light might come from the Orient—a thing which has not been happening to any effective degree. We have reached a moment at which the peoples of Asia cannot understand either their Marxism or their dreams of autonomy, either their secular ideals or their governmental machinery, without digging into the history of Western Europe, just as we have to look for our origins in classical Greece and Biblical Israel. The achievements of the ancient Chinese in natural science and technology may outshine those of Western antiquity, but their modern successors, whether they use electricity or move into atomic physics, must trace the origins of their modern science back to Sir Isaac Newton and the Scientific Revolution of the West. Marxism can Westernize Asia more radically in a few decades than Western Europe had managed to do in the course of centuries. But our science and our secularism have proved to be more easily communicable to other continents than either Christianity itself or the subtler virtues and more imponderable ideals of our civilization.

If Western Europe has lost its global predominance, the religion which inspired so much of our culture has long been losing its dominion even in the countries where once it reigned supreme. The Christian Church has been driven from that general presidency which it once enjoyed in European society as a whole—driven from that majority position which once enabled it to gain so many monopolies and priorities and special advantages for itself. The time has come when Christianity, for example, must compete on fairly equal terms with all the other gospels, creeds and ideologies which now do battle for the possession of the souls of men. Many Christians still allow their thinking to be unconsciously shaped by the memory or the survivals of that ancient system of privilege. Their minds are still governed by a traditional notion of the part which the Church should play in an organized society and a developing civilization. They expect to have the dice loaded in their favor either by governments or by educational systems or by the continuing power of social convention. In this way, in an important transition period, they reduce their chances of influencing by other means a world with which they are too much at cross purposes. There is nothing in New Testament Christianity which authorizes us to claim from Providence that things should be made easy for us in the way to which the Church has been accustomed. Nothing in the religion itself gives us the right to expect that even in the cause of the Gospel we should enjoy the alliance of political authorities, mundane systems, vested interests and organized force. If Christianity has in some respects come into a period of decline, one of the primary reasons for this is the fact that at a crucial moment in history it chose to make this alliance with power, and has clung to it with pathetic consequences for fifteen hundred years. One of the reasons why it contributes less than we might wish to the problems of our time is the fact that its traditional systems of thought have been so intertwined with that mundane order of things which it accepted as its ally. All this has long provoked a profound resentment in well-meaning men who do not always understand that the Christian faith is not necessarily allied to the regimes and systems to which churchmen have come to attach it. Even today there is no doubt that this initial resentment has the effect of preventing some people from opening their minds to the Christian message itself. In considering the prospects of Christianity, we should be wise, therefore, to begin by throwing out of our minds all the ancient, illicit dreams of power. In spite of the remnants of the old system which still survive, we should be closer to reality if we pictured Christianity against a pagan background, Christianity trying to keep its light shining in a hostile world. It is better to think of Christianity as it was in the earliest centuries of its history than to be deluded by the kinds of power that it has enjoyed in the very long intervening period.

Not merely in the West, but over the entire globe, there must come sooner or later a dissolution of the traditional hereditary systems of officially imposed or conventionally accepted religions. Our natural science, our technology, our rationalism and the superficial parts of our secular culture which are easily transmissible are already producing a remarkable transformation in other continents. They are bound to have the same dissolvent effects upon the traditional systems of India, Japan and China as they have had upon the Christian tradition and heritage of European countries. However profoundly rooted they may seem to be, and however solid they may appear at the moment, the religions of the East are threatened by the same kind of dislodgment which our traditional Western religious order has suffered in recent generations. This means that, sooner or later, Christianity will be faced over still larger areas of the globe with the very problem that we confront at home—the spectacle of modern secularism. In this sense, too, it is the globe as a whole which is now becoming "Westernized."

We must not close our eyes to the fact that this development, and even the universal spread of secularism, though it will present to Christianity the greatest test in its history, will also offer it the greatest opportunity. Secularism itself may be very hostile at the moment, for it still resents the special privileges that churches so long possessed and continue to try to maintain. But secularism is a fickle, flexible and amorphous thing, always unhappy, always flitting like a lost soul in the world, always tragically unsure of itself. Indeed it is always hankering to discover a god or a *mystique* or a form of self-immolation—liable to sink back into astrologies, theosophies and dark superstitions. It is arguable that when resentments are past and there is less obstruction from ecclesiastical tradition, Europeans and Americans will be able to listen to the Gospel with minds much more open than at the present day. There are many young men who, though they apparently have little interest in party politics, seem to be galvanized in a remarkable way when there is a public issue that is ethical in character. Sometimes they seem almost to be lying in wait for a morally challenging cause, but unable to convince themselves that they will find this in anything so conventional as Christianity. In other continents, moreover, the secularism which is being produced is a secularism that has been imported from the West so that in certain respects it is shaped somewhat to the mind of the West. It is bound to be more vulnerable in the long run to the Christian challenge than the stony block of Islam has been during a period of well over a thousand years. One of the countries in which primitive Christianity could make little headway was the Holy Land, because there it was confronted by the solid resistance of an entrenched Judaism. Areas where another religion has been established in a monolithic way and on a hereditary footing have always presented a special problem to Christian missions.

On the other hand, if we go back to the beginnings of Christian history, the realm which seemed to lie wide open for the advance of the Church was the tumultuous, highly urbanized, highly civilized Roman Empire in the earliest centuries after the time of Christ. Here, from an unpromising beginning, the Gospel achieved the most wonderful of its large-scale victories, doing it by the process of individual conversion, even when at times it was opposed by the might of the Roman government. The one right which Christians can properly claim is a free and mobile world in which the Gospel can be preached and men can make the decision to be converted. They are not to despair even when they are being cheated of this right, but it is particularly incumbent on them both to demand this freedom for themselves and grant it to everybody else. In reality they ought to be opposed to monolithic systems whether of hereditary Communism or hereditary Islam; and for the same reason when they themselves establish such systems, and use force or the law to maintain them, they can only be excused if a primitive state of civilization makes authentic autonomy impossible for the human beings concerned. Societies which are Communist or Christian or Mohammedan by mere custom or compulsion represent an interim stage in the history of civilization. Against such systems as these, the Western type of freedom which developed out of what were originally Christian demands and claims ought to be valued by the Christian more than the alliance of any regime or government. The conflict of religions in the Roman Empire was an impressive affair, but was nothing compared with the conflict of religions which, sooner or later, is going to take place on a global scale. Those who really have faith will ask nothing from the world but freedom to communicate their beliefs; and in a free world, even if it is a highly secularized world, they will look to the future conflict of religions as the greatest and most exhilarating of opportunities.

In both secular and religious affairs, therefore, a world which has too long been contracted and kept in darkness is opening out to a wider kind of freedom; and we of the West too often feel that this is a reverse for us, and that the future is closing in on us. The whole globe is in a sense being Westernized and the cultural leadership of the West is now more remarkable than we had usually imagined would ever be possible. Christianity itself is being disengaged from regimes and mundane systems which had so long helped to constrict it and to make it look like a regional religion. We waste time when we regret forms of political predominance and even forms of religious predominance, for in reality we know that these things are inconsistent with our own fundamental ideas. There is now emerging the kind of world which successive generations of our predecessors had hoped for, and had anxiously attempted to produce. In both politics and religion we may go sadly wrong if we are concerned to be looking for safeguards instead of looking for opportunities in this new situation. It is possible that we envisage the immediate future with minds too constricted by fear.

Our predecessors struggled for generations to secure a regime of liberty, and earlier in the twentieth century there was a feeling that at last we were entering the Promised Land. In more recent decades there has been a reaction, and sometimes it has been younger men who have been dismayed by the spectacle of modern individualism and the appearance of intellectual anarchy on all sides. Some have shrunk from the responsibility of making decisions, or proclaimed their defeat in the face of the problems of life. They have confessed that they hankered for authoritarianism and for an orthodoxy, whether like that of the Middle Ages or like that of Communism. Freedom sometimes produces untidiness, but the democratic world is greatly enriched by the sheer variety of its intellectual manifestations. In the long run, society is much more flexible and dynamic if original ideas (or original combinations of ideas) are continually sprouting up from thousands of independent centers. Where we have a vast and uniform organization, everything is liable to collapse at once if the director of the machine makes a single mistake; and perhaps in democracies themselves there is less danger from the chaos of divergent opinions than from those areas which provide a given age with its fashionable obsessions and its generally accepted ideas. These latter are the things which future historians sometimes find it so difficult to explain because so many irrational factors are involved in them. We are even wrong to be afraid to see multiple centers of foreign policy in the world—India taking its independent course, the Arabs flirting with Russia when it seems profitable, and Yugoslavia oscillating between East and West. International affairs are happier when they are conducted from many free and autonomous centers, happiest of all when the small states are able to have an independent role. The strain is too severe and too unremitting when the balance of the whole globe depends on the tension between two or three great giants; and in such a situation the whole of the free world may become too dependent on the ability of the United States to get through without making a single serious mistake. One solitary global government, besides being under unspeakable pressures all the time, would mean that disaster was universalized if through some single great misjudgment the world was carried in a wrong direction. Rigid organization, in spite of its short-term success, not only tends to cramp the human beings within it, but freezes and becomes the prisoner of itself. The ideal of the democracies—if it is to be consistent with the principles out of which democratic ideas emerged—must be a mobile world, with everything on ball bearings, ready (in modern society) for agile changes of direction. It is arguable that at some point in the twentieth century—perhaps during the First World War, or earlier still—the liberal-minded people of the world were not liberal-minded enough. At some point we may have been too distrustful of freedom, too dismayed by the kind of world that we saw developing, and too forgetful of the fact that the processes of time, which bring some unexpected ills, also sometimes bring unexpected cures for other ills. In all this, once again, we see a certain evidence of the dominion of fear.

The question arises, therefore, whether, in the present situation, the Western democracies can expect either to save themselves or to rescue the world save by a policy of unusual audacity. It is not clear that they can afford to show less audacity—or, in other words, to have less faith in their ideals—than the Communists have been showing. Apart from the fact that the position and the policy of a Metternich are so weak and unconvincing, any mere defense of the *status quo* against the rising forces of the twentieth century is a negation of Western ideals. We should consider it a justifiable cause of reproach against anybody else who tried to undertake it; and the policy has a depressing psychological effect upon those who are trying to follow it. Anything like a struggle for the older type of imperialism is calculated to lead amongst ourselves to just those authoritarian developments which the Communists regard as necessary consequences of the policy. In reality, the stage is now set for a conflict of ideals in the world at large; and if we are too preoccupied even with questions of power—too intent upon the requirements of a hypothetical war—we may be unfitting ourselves for what is only too likely to turn out to be the main issue in the present decade of conflict. At the stage which has now been reached, our *status quo* is liable to be changed without any resort to actual war—without any opportunity of inserting even the hydrogen bomb to stop the change.

It has always been true that the men who were defending Western ideals were bound to be in alliance with men who intended to defend only Western vested interests. The two have been parting company at times, however, and we do not always sufficiently grasp the fact that we are going to be in a position in which we can only defend our ideals by extending them in a more dynamic manner to other parts of the world. I think it is open to us to secure victory for our ideals, but I am not clear that we shall be able to hold on to our vested interests, whatever policy we adopt. And one of our chief dangers may be that we ourselves, by an excessive materialism, will calculate too much, and rely too much, on power in the physical and brutal sense of the word. Democracies sometimes hate to have to think of war; but when they do turn to the idea they have shown more than once in the twentieth century that they quickly become headstrong, forgetting the limits of what power can actually achieve. Our great danger is that we might lose our ideals in the process of having to fight for them, or we might allow that process to make us become more and more like the very thing we first set out to destroy. It speaks well for the wisdom and good will of those who govern us that democracy and liberty have suffered as little as they have done in England and America, where also it would be possible for us to have too little faith in our principles of freedom.

When we think of the Hapsburg Empire in the age of Metternich, we, who have seen the distresses of that part of Europe since 1918, can well picture the more imaginative policy which we wish that empire could have pursued in the face of the rising forces of the nineteenth century. It is we who must be out to change the *status quo* in the world, and even to be ahead of Soviet Russia, which may not always wish to see the genuine independence and autonomy of certain countries, and may not want to have a power vacuum filled. For this reason we ought to confront ourselves with a question which is fast becoming the crucial one and is surely going to be inescapable. We have to ask ourselves whether there is anything that Russia has to offer to the less-developed or uncommitted regions of the world —and particularly to the populations concerned—that we ourselves are unable to offer them. It is liable to be a serious question for us, because any self-deceptions of ours will not deceive the rest of the world, and some of our self-deceptions are perhaps proving their fallaciousness already. What is required of us is that we should offer not less than all that Russia can offer, with the benefits of freedom and autonomy thrown in as an extra—always remembering that autonomy in regard to foreign policy is a thing for which peoples will sacrifice other freedoms, and deny themselves prosperity, a thing they will refuse to exchange for money. In truth, we do not for a moment believe that in the long run the Russians want the Arabs to attain real freedom or genuine autonomy or independent power. Here the West can have the advantage; for on the one hand we cannot (on our own principles) deny these things to the Arabs, while on the other hand we can say that they are things which cannot come quickly enough for us. We would support the rights of Israel in the same way; but it is not clear that Israel would be threatened if she did not give so convenient a handle to Arab nationalism while this nationalism is still in its insurgent stage. And if we cannot do for the undeveloped peoples all that they might want or need, at least we can be careful not to be caught committed to nations and systems which, on the almost unanimous evidence of our own newspapers, must discredit our cause and make us appear as the enemies of freedom. A new kind of warfare is installed, and we now have to adjust our minds to it: namely, the competition (and, in some respects, the race) between Western Democracy and Eastern Communism as positive missionary ideals—alternative ways of producing what must now be regarded as inescapable changes in the world at large. Nothing could be more injurious to our cause than any suggestion that we dare not allow any of the peoples of the world to decide for themselves between these two ideals—to decide even whether they will have a revolution or not. Our role is rather to hold the ring for them, or at least to remove the obstructions to the identification and achievement of the thing which they, as peoples, really want.

In religion it is equally possible that too many fears constrict us and that nothing will serve save the greatest audacity. Over thirty years ago, the churches brought to a climax a liberal movement which in certain ways was extravagant. It was as though Christians had come to have an inferiority complex and wished to reduce their religion to the common sense of the modern world. On the other hand, in their reaction against these mistakes, churchmen since that time may have become overtimid, so that they are sometimes in danger of closing up their minds. Protestants, forgetting the greatness of their own traditions, have envied or mimicked Catholicism, or set out to show that they were as "Catholic" as the followers of Rome. The role of tradition in religion is a subtle matter, and can be made hard and rigid where it ought to be sympathetic and flexible. It is possible to have a hankering after orthodoxy and conformity, and to make this a constant basis of reference, in such a way as to check the adventures of the mind. On questions which concern the relations between the Church and the world too great a solicitude for the conventional churchgoer may be based on prudential calculations which are too narrow, since they take no account of the importance of the concealed losses that attend the policy. In general it might be said that if the liberal churchmen went wrong, their fault did not lie in their intellectual audacity but sprang rather from what must have been a defect on the spiritual side. Sometimes the people who have shown the greatest depth and the firmest apprehension in spiritual matters have in fact been the ones who have displayed the greatest audacity, not in discovering what is "modern," but in seizing upon what is timeless and disengaging it from the accidents of Western history. For centuries now, churchmen have been presenting the appearance of intellectual retreat because they confused the eternal with the merely ancient, and held on too long to the things which in reality were only the product of time. Three centuries ago, their religious ideas were so entangled with the whole Aristotelian picture of the cosmos that they found it difficult to see how faith itself could survive if the ancient cosmology was overthrown. Ultimately they could not avoid presenting the spectacle of intellectual retreat; but there need have been no retreat, for the separation of religion from a particular view or theory of the physical universe merely forced them to take a firmer grasp on the things that are spiritual. For this reason religious people most of all ought to face the challenge of a new age without the constrictions produced by fear.

A close comparison of ecclesiastical utterances between 1914 and 1918 on the subject of the First World War might surprise us by its revelation of the unconscious ways in which churches—even unestablished or nonconformist churches—become tied to particular states or regimes. The principles of the Christian religion, and even identifiable Biblical texts, lay behind much of the movement toward liberty for a number of centuries; but churches, too unaware of the way they had become attached to the existing *status quo,* often resisted the actualization of the ideals of freedom. They left it to the nonconformists in one age, and the "lapsed Christians" in another age, to play a particularly important part in the history of modern liberty. This fact stands as an interesting comment on the subtle importance of the unconscious relationships which can be established between religion and the existing order. It would seem that the nonconformists (through being an almost professional "opposition") and the "lapsed Christians" (through their break with the Church) were released from conventionalities, released for a more radical development of the implications of Christian charity in the world. The problem of the relations between the Church and the world may even be becoming more important and more acute as the twentieth century develops, and perhaps holds more concealed dangers for the Protestant than for the Catholic. The main point of difficulty lies in our incapacity to stand outside ourselves—our unconscious way of identifying our religion with a regime and an existing order which now appear to us only too self-evidently right. We even forget that there was a time when our Christian predecessors thought that the wrongness of our present order was equally self-evident. It is perhaps even the case that a subtle secret sympathy with the *status quo* now almost robs nonconformity of its historical role in England, making it no longer a body predisposed to opposition (and in this sense perhaps inclined to uncharitableness)—no longer so intent upon measuring the existing order of things by a standard outside that order itself.

The saints always seem to have an answer to the problem of disengaging the essentials of the New Testament faith, and of the spiritual life, from their entanglement with particular times and particular regions. Those in the Roman Catholic Church who are otherworldly no doubt come nearer to the answer than those amongst the Protestants who sometimes identify Christianity too closely with Western ideals or with what in England is called "the public school spirit." One can hardly measure the misfortune that would result if, through the continents of Asia and Africa, Christianity were too closely identified with our mundane systems, and associated with either the vested interests or the political ambitions of the Western powers. The awakening of a great part of the world, and its new consciousness of its adult status, make it more important than ever to release the Christian faith itself from that large fringe of associated ideas and prejudices which are merely the result of its Western history. The revolutionary character of the present world situation does not call for the kind of Christianity which in a settled world associates itself with the defense of the existing order. It calls for the other kind of Christianity, the insurgent type, which goes back to first principles and measures the present order of things against these.

Here there arises an ethical point which has already been discussed in certain of its aspects, and of which we must say that at least it closely concerns the Christian, whether it affects anybody else or not. We know that for us, when we are discussing these matters, it is the principle of love which is the final touchstone and which reigns in the universe, keeping the planets in motion and holding the solar system in a network of harmonious relationships. Only, the love is not impersonal—it attaches itself not to mere objects or even abstract nouns but to human beings, who are always the supreme values (always ends and never merely means) in the realm of mundane things. Love is not to be subordinated to a kind of justice which is seen as an impersonal balance, hanging in the heavens—a balance for the rectification of which human beings are to be immolated and, if necessary, the world set on fire. Justice is important, but it is a dubious affair when administered by men, and dubious most of all in international politics, where each party is judging his own cause. And justice at its highest is not to be sundered from mercy, and it does not supersede love—it is rather a subordinate system within the order of love itself. Men have fought in the name of justice for the rights of property, but in the course of time the operation of love has revised the rights of property themselves—revised, amongst human beings, the actual conception of what is just. If this has been true in the internal life of states and societies—within modern England, for example—it is equally relevant and more urgently needed, particularly at the present day, in international affairs. While we are proclaiming our rights, and insisting upon their fairness in the eyes of the law, the outside world is calling upon us to revise our notion of what is right, our conception of justice itself. In the days when we were the rising powers, both England and America called on the defenders of the *status quo* to make just this kind of revision, and similarly the liberals once demanded it from Metternich. Even when we feel ourselves to be just and fair, we are being called upon to revise the very standards on which we were brought up, the very standards by which justice is measured. Here it is not by any means only the Communists who are against us. In a conjuncture which makes such a new kind of call upon us, there is need for the love which is the equivalent of creative imagination.

Index

Abdulgani, Ruslan, 29
Abyssinia, 101
Acton, Lord, 17
African, 29, 30, 101, 103–105, 118
Aggression, 25, 31, 33–34, 51, 70, 73–74, 86–87, 96
Algeria, 32, 42, 96
Arabs, the, 16, 28, 30, 52, 101–104, 112, 115
Armaments, 86, 89–98
Asia, 29, 101–104, 118

Bacon, Francis, 51
Balance of power, 50–52, 62, 70, 112
Balkans, the, 97, 102
Bomb, Hydrogen, 88, 91–98, 113
Burke, Edmund, 76

Calvinism, 67, 71
Capernaum, 24
Carlyle, Thomas, 46
Catholicism, 63–67, 75–76, 98, 116, 118
Charity, law of, 23, 118–19
China, 36, 62, 90, 105–106, 108
Christendom, 101, 105
Christian, the "lapsed," 18, 68, 117–18
Christianity and Christians, 13, 15–18, 23–24, 28, 37, 64, 68, 75–76, 98, 102, 106–11, 117–19
Columbus, Christopher, 101–102
Communism and Communists, 16, 23–24, 33, 36–37, 42, 61, 70–72, 74, 77, 87–88, 90–91, 93–94, 97, 104–106, 110–11, 113, 115
Conscience, Rights of, 18, 65, 68–69
Constantinople, Fall of, 102
Cujus regio ejus religio, 66, 72

Democracy and Democrats, 23, 37, 42, 50, 71–72, 75–78, 91, 114–15
De Valera, Eamon, 27
Diplomacy, function of, 74, 76

Eden, Sir Anthony, 41
Empire, British, 31, 34, 36, 103
Erasmus, 68
Europe (Western) in Global History, 28, 101–106

Fitzsimons, M. A., 29
Force, the rôle of, 33, 98, 114
France, 34, 49, 61, 65–66, 75–76, 84, 86
Freedom, 17–18, 33, 38, 44–47, 56, 76, 89, 91, 96–98, 104–105, 110–11, 113–17
Freedom, religious, 65–69

Galileo, 53–56
Gama, Vasco da, 101
Geneva, 71
George III, 32
Germany, 34, 47, 62, 70, 73, 75, 85–88, 90
Gladstone, W. E., 26, 28
Gordon Riots, 82
Grey, Sir Edward, 84

Habsburgs, The, 36, 48–49, 75, 114
History, laws in, 53–55
History, processes of, 13, 45, 49, 61, 63, 66, 69, 72–74, 89, 97–98
Hitler, 36, 41, 51, 85, 88, 92–93
Hobbes, Thomas, 84–85
Huguenots, 65
Hungary, 102

121

Imperialism, 28, 30–33, 35–36, 103–104, 113

India and Indians, 28, 31, 101, 103, 108, 112

Individual, the importance in history of the, 44–47

Individualism, 15–18

Indonesia, 29

International order or system, 76, 78, 90

Iraq, 72

Ireland, 26-29

Islam, 101–102, 109–10

Israel, 106, 115

Jacobin Dictatorship, 37

Japan, 108

Judaism, 109

Judgments, moral, 23–28

Justice, 94, 119–20

Khrushchev, 63

League of Nations, 31

Liberty, *see under* Freedom

Liberum veto, 31–32

Louis XIV, 84

Luther, Martin, 63, 68

Marxism, 71, 106

Mazarin, Cardinal, 84

Metternich, 32, 71, 113–14, 120

Moral factors in international politics, 30, 38

Morality, political, 15–16, 23–24, 27–28, 48–49

Moscow, 71, 86

Napoleon I, 53, 56, 86

Nasser, Colonel, 41

Newton, Sir Isaac, 106

Nonconformists, 117–18

Norway, 85

Nuclear weapons, 30, 88–98, 113

Personality, 15–18

Pharisees, the, 24, 26

Pitt, William, the Younger, 76

Poland, 66

Portuguese, the, 101

Protestantism and Protestants, 63–67, 70–71, 74–77, 98, 116, 118

Ranke, Leopold von, 42

Renaissance, the, 102

Responsibility, human, 16–18, 25–26, 44–47

Review of Politics, The, 29

Revolution, 13, 32, 48, 54–56, 62–63, 71, 73, 77, 82, 103–105, 116

Revolution, French, 36–37, 46, 63, 76, 82, 85–86

Revolution, Russian, 46, 63, 86

Richelieu, Cardinal, 56, 75

Robespierre, Maximilian, 63, 82

Roman Empire, 102, 110

Russia and the Russians, 30, 33–34, 36–37, 62–63, 71–72, 86, 88, 90, 93–94, 112, 114–15

Science, Natural, 41, 52–54, 67, 108

Scott, Sir Walter, 56

Secularism, 106, 108–10

Security, the problem of, 85–86

Simon, Sir John, 26

Stalin, 63, 87

State, the idea of the, 15

Status quo, revision of the, 28–33, 35–38, 48, 50, 71, 113–14, 120

Suez Crisis, the, 29, 96

Toleration, 65–69, 74–76

Toynbee, Arnold, 43–44, 51–52

Treaties, 18–19, 29, 31

Tudor, Mary, 23

Turks, Ottoman, 101–103

Uniqueness of historical events, 42–45

United Nations Organization, 28

United States, 75, 86–87, 90, 105, 112, 114

Versailles, Treaty of, (1919) 30–31, 41

Victoria, Queen, 26, 28

Vienna, 102

Vienna, Treaty of, 41

Violence, the resort to, 26–28, 32–
  33
Wars of Religion, 63–69, 76, 84,
  98

Whig historians, 27
World War I, 33, 48–50, 85, 87–
  88, 112–13, 117
Yugoslavia, 112